TIPS FOR THE SAVVY TRAVELER

by
Deborah Burns
and
Sarah May Clarkson

A Storey Publishing Book

STOREY

STOREY COMMUNICATIONS, INC.
POWNAL, VERMONT 05261

Acknowledgments

The authors would like to thank the following people for their contributions: Constance Oxley, Cindy McFarland, Jack and Annie Archambault, Pam Art, Susan Auerbach, Janet Auster, Kingsley Barham, Sharon Bray, Jim and Joan Burns, Rain Burns, Beth Connolly, Riva Enteen, Judie Evrard, Susan Fuhr, Cyndi Garrison, Bernie Graney, Sheila and Jack Higgins, Jan Keep, Margaret F. Lally, Jill Mason, Ellen McCauley McGarty, Catherine McHugh, Tom McHugh, Peter Meyers, Margot Page, Ellen Scott of the Hoosac Travel Agency, Mary Smith, Bob Spicer, and Martha and John Storey.

Cover Illustration by Kimble Pendleton Mead
Cover Design by Leslie Morris Noyes
Text Design by Wanda Harper
Typesetting by Hemmings Publishing

Printed in the United States by Hamilton Printing Company

First Printing, May, 1987

Library of Congress Catalog Card Number: 86-43042
Library of Congress Cataloging-in-Publication Data

Burns, Deborah.
  Tips for the savvy traveler.

  "A Storey Publishing book."
  Includes index.
  1. Travel. I. Clarkson, Sarah May. II. Title
G151.B87 1987   910'.2'02   86-43042
ISBN 0-88266-464-6 (pbk.)

DEDICATION

From Deborah:
To my globetrotting grandmothers, my original inspiration; and to Thomas and Sean

From Sarah:
To K.R.C.
Soulmate, traveling companion, and buddy

      The world of travel is constantly expanding. We have tried to be as thorough as possible in this book, but our knowledge is limited by our own experiences and those of the people we've talked to. Part of the joy of travel is making discoveries and solving problems yourself! If you have any tips or suggestions that you feel are especially useful, please write us in care of the publisher. If we include them in the next edition of this book, we will give you credit.

The Authors

TABLE OF CONTENTS

PREFACE

by Martha Storey, Associate Publisher

My earliest memories are of travel. My Texan daddy would pile the four of us kids into an old Nash Rambler at our home in Texhoma, right smack on the Oklahoma border, and we'd set sail for Corpus Christi to visit relatives.

Daddy, an engineer and an efficiency expert, didn't believe in spending a lot of money on restaurants or motels, so when we'd leave on one of those 700-mile excursions, we might as well have been confined in a NASA capsule, embarking on a nonstop 25-hour trip to outer space. He packed our underwear in our sneakers to save room, and he even built a bed in the back of the Rambler so Mother could sleep while we drove.

When we did have to stay overnight somewhere, it would be in a comfortable rooming house, rather than in a fancy hotel. Travelers have rediscovered that today, and the "bed and breakfast" business is booming. When Daddy agreed to a meal out, it would be at a cafeteria, rather than at a more expensive restaurant, and I still remember the taste of the homemade barbecued chicken and warm apple pie.

Mother was the navigator, steward, and trip psychologist. She could make our voyages bearable, if not quite fun. She'd bring out little surprises as the journey progressed — Life Savers in Amarillo, a game of license plates in Lubbock, some soda pop in San Antonio — and while she'd never think of herself as a "savvy" traveler, I did and still do. On our trips, and during our frequent moves, Mother taught us all to be organized, patient, and prepared. She encouraged us to entertain ourselves, and to have a dime in our pocket and a friend or relative in every city to call.

When my husband John and I embarked on an 18-month living experience in Italy and France, I needed all of Mother's patience and savvy. On our first night in Bologna, a city of 400,000 off the tourist trail,

I cried after seeing our substandard hotel room with no view but lots of Fiat 500 street noise and exhaust.

We went out to dinner at a nearby *trattoria,* and laboriously studied the Italian menu and seeming outrageous prices. We were overcharged for tough veal, nondescript pasta, and a strange, fruity wine, but we couldn't negotiate because of our language inadequacy. We paid and left. I cried again.

Things got better as I mastered a few phrases of Italian, got the conversion rates down cold, and moved out of that hotel. John, meanwhile, was meeting challenges of his own. After we found an *appartamento* in a modest neighborhood, I sent him down to get some vegetables for dinner. I wished him luck as he headed out, dictionary in hand, looking very American in his Bermuda shorts, white T-shirt and sneakers. From the kitchen window I could see him, in front of the tiny *groceria* across the street, negotiating furiously. He appeared at the door a few minutes later with three gigantic brown paper bags in his arms and a sheepish grin on his face. "I was able to get two kilos of beans for only 100 lire!" he said proudly. We had beans for a while, and John worked on his conversions.

We learned the importance of keeping receipts when our landlady insisted that the wool Oriental rug we had proudly purchased at the Saturday morning flea market was hers!

We learned the way summer rentals work in Paris, when the owner of a beautiful Montparnasse apartment told us it would cost $1,500. "For the summer!" I asked. "Yes, for the summer," she answered. We decided to take it, and she asked for the $4,500 in advance. "What $4,500?" I asked. "For the summer rental," she answered. I learned, painfully, what *par mois* ("by the month") meant.

Then there was the time in Singapore when, vexed by a head cold and a long day of travel, I went down for a steam bath and massage. As I relaxed in the steam bath, I heard an explosion of laughter among the female attendants. Into the steam bath with me stepped a male, 300-pound, Sumo-type Singaporean, *au naturel!* I pulled my towel up firmly, smiled politely, and moved on.

From my own experiences I've learned that travel can't be totally predictable, and that's part of the fun. Deborah Burns and Sarah May Clarkson, my friends and the authors of *Tips for the Savvy Traveler,* have gone to great lengths to uncover the tips, tricks, and suggestions that will help you avoid hassles, to stay on top of your trip, and to get help when you need it. The book has helped me, and I suspect it will help you, too.

I applaud their efforts, and I wish you enjoyable trips, "with the breeze at your back and the sun in your face."

April, 1987

CHAPTER ONE

SETTING A COURSE

If you go only once around the room, you are wiser than he who stands still.

— Estonian proverb

You don't need a lot of money to travel well. Too much money can actually make your trip less interesting, especially when you're traveling in places like Mexico and Asia. Nor do you need to be young and carefree — some of the happiest travelers we've ever seen were members of a senior group, the "Gadabouts," whom we met on a ferry going up the British Columbia coast to Alaska.

We believe the single most important ingredient of successful travel is a positive attitude — the confidence to handle any situation that comes up and a cheerful self-reliance that helps you turn disappointments into benefits. (So maybe you didn't get as good a fare as the person sitting next to you on the plane — next time you'll know. Maybe this summer *was* the worst weather Europe has had in 100 years — but it was something remarkable you shared with the locals.)

Travel is one of the best educations you can get, especially if you try to speak the language, master the currency, eat the food, and support the local arts. Not only will you learn about the places you visit, but you'll also understand your own country better, by seeing it from another point of view. If you can embrace the foreignness of a place with enthusiasm, many things will come into perspective: your life, your work, and your place in the world.

Some people find their best side comes out under the particular conditions of travel. You may love being in charge of your own destiny and having all the essentials of life in one suitcase. Or you may be apprehensive — about the security of your home, your health, or possible loneliness en route.

We hope this book will help make your travel successful — free of problems and full of discovery. While we were writing it, certain ideas kept surfacing, and we thought it made sense to gather these in some prominent place in the book. These tips seem to us to be the most important, overall, for successful travel. They are grouped more or less chronologically, that is, in the order that you might use them.

■ Start making plans early. The earlier you can commit yourself to your travel plans, the more options you'll have, and the better the deals will be. Be firm and decide early on about transportation arrangements to your destination.

■ Read as much as possible about the place you're visiting. Browse in your public library, read all available guidebooks, and explore background information (the Greek myths, for example, if you're going to the Aegean). Try to get a sense of the culture, the politics and the religion. (See Chapter 23, "Useful Addresses," for names of guides to travel reading.)

■ Travel light.

■ Ask for a discount or you won't get it.

■ Stay alert — read the fine print, listen to announcements, and hang onto your possessions.

■ Don't try to do everything. Slow down. Build into your schedule some time to relax, to play, to be spontaneous (especially if you're traveling with kids). Flexibility and a reasonable pace will let you respond when something terrific turns up — a new friend invites you to visit his country home in France, for example, or there's room for you on a chartered sailboat cruising the Hawaiian islands. (This doesn't contradict with the first tip, above — be firm about your major transportation arrangements, but flexible once you get there.)

■ Focus on just a few places instead of many. Even in Europe, where things are relatively close together, travel time eats up your precious vacation. Instead stay in one area and discover its many dimensions — people, places, views, walks, various historical eras, museums, music, food, ancient monuments, and so on.

■ Be discreet — don't flaunt your money. Carry your valuables on your person or keep them in the hotel safe.

■ Get a map of your destination and become familiar with it — both for safety and for information.

■ Walk. Nothing compares with it as the best way to see the world.

■ Bring sturdy, comfortable walking shoes, well broken in.

■ Get up and out early to see how the day begins — whether you're in Boston or Bangkok.

■ Try to speak the language.

■ Beware of deals that seem too good to be true — they probably are.

■ Visit people that live there.

■ Once you're on your way, get your nose out of the guidebook. Guidebooks are for studying ahead of time.

■ Follow through after your trip. If a service was particularly good or bad, let the supplier know. Communicate with the new friends you made.

WHERE TO GO

This is the easy part. You may take a trip for the sun or for the people you know there. You may want to see something spectacular or something exotic. You may be seeking adventure — or peace and quiet.

Start planning when you first get the travel itch. Send away for brochures (see Chapter 23, "Useful Addresses," for addresses of state and national tourist offices). Ask yourself what you and your partner or family most like to do — visit people? have adventures? go to the beach?

Plan your trip so that everyone will have fun, including the kids. (See Chapter 18, "Traveling with Children.")

Decide what mode of transportation you will use, and begin scouting for good deals.

TRAVEL AGENTS

Look around until you find a good travel agent. A professional can be a valuable resource, sharing experiences and expertise, helping you plan and book a vacation, finding big discounts and special deals, and giving you the latest information on everything from new resorts to possible airport hang-ups — all at no cost to you.

Travel agents are paid a commission by all the various suppliers with which they do business — airlines, hotels, cruise lines, railroads, and vacation resorts. The only time travel agents may charge the consumer directly is if they plan a very complicated itinerary or if they arrange a large tour group; in the latter case part of the total expense will be a modest travel agent surcharge that will be paid equally by all members of the group. Some travel agents do not promote discount flights, because they do not receive a commission on them.

If you keep trying, however, you will find one of those very special travel agents who are real artists, who love their work and are good at it — canny, patient, and imaginative, with a good memory and good computer skills.

You will be able to tell if you have found a competent travel agent by the degree of interest and care taken with you as a customer. Did he or she conduct a "personal profile" to determine what your needs and desires are, and what your situation and budget will allow? Did he or she ask intelligent questions? If you asked a question that could not be answered immediately, was there a promise that an answer would be forthcoming? Most of all, if you felt that you were treated courteously and professionally, chances are you have made a good choice.

Travel agents deal with all kinds of customers, and will most often be glad just to sit and give you some vacation ideas and prices. You should never feel pressured by a travel agent — if you do, you're with the wrong person.

Make sure that you tell your travel agent you want **the best deal possible.** He or she should take into account special low fares, unusual deals that will get you to your destination more cheaply (along with a package tour, for instance, with which you would part upon reaching your destination), and the time it takes to transfer passengers and luggage from airline to airline.

In addition to the standard functions of a travel agent (developing itineraries, making reservations, issuing tickets) he or she may also be able to tell you what you may need in the way of immunizations, how to go about obtaining a passport or foreign visa, where the car rental agency is in relation to the terminal at the airport you are planning to use, whether you should buy trip insurance, and if it's really true that the *Norway* is so big it has to carry about 100,000 pieces of china.

FINDING A TRAVELING PARTNER

If you find you do not enjoy traveling on your own, you may decide to hook up with another single traveler. Or you may choose to travel as a partnership to avail yourself of better deals (half of a double room is usually cheaper than a single room).

When you decide to travel with another person, you may want to find out the answers to certain questions (see box). Most important is to agree that you're financially independent of one another. Be sure that your partner is responsible with money, and won't turn to you for help. Next most important is that each respects what the other wants to do. Try also to get a sense of their personal habits — are they compatible with yours? — and how they react in a crisis. The answers to these questions may not be reasons not to travel with a person; they are simply useful to know in advance. Flexibility and amiability are most important.

The best of friends can turn into enemies in the close quarters and constant companionship of a shared trip. Trips can actually be ruined when two people don't get along. Your memory of the Louvre, for example, might be completely colored by the fact that your traveling partner was sulking. If you have good communication, however, problems are solvable.

One way to avoid problems is to schedule regular time apart — one day a week, for example, when you part after breakfast and go off alone, with a rendezvous at dinner or after to share your experiences. This way you can each do what you really want — shop, go to a museum, or sit all day in a sidewalk cafe — without worrying about a less enthusiastic partner. You'll rediscover your own perceptions, make your own decisions and set your own pace. When you meet up with each other again, you'll have new insights to share and a new appreciation for each other.

THINGS TO KNOW ABOUT A TRAVELING PARTNER

■ How do they handle finances — are they extravagant or irresponsible, or do they spend as little money as possible?

■ Does one aspect of the trip interest them particularly — shopping, mountain climbing, going to discos, going to museums, eating well, getting a tan, having a love affair — and does that coincide with your expectations?

■ How do they react in a crisis?

■ Are their personal habits compatible with yours? Are they neat or messy? Are they night owls or early risers? Are they punctual? Are you? (Will one of you always be pushing the other to catch that train?)

■ How will you resolve problems? Will one of you assume leadership and make decisions or will you decide things together?

■ Are they timid, adventurous, daring, or fool-hardy? (Will one of you be always holding back?)

■ Do they meet people easily?

■ Is one of you good at a particular task (navigating, speaking the language, bargaining), and do you want to divide up such responsibilities?

SHARING EXPENSES

A successful way we've found to manage finances when traveling in a group, especially in a car, is to **pool our money in a "kitty."** Each person contributes the same amount of money, and all expenses are paid from the kitty. When the fund gets low, it's replenished. At the end of the trip, what's left is split equally. You don't have to argue over bills or worry about each person's share of gas. Keep track of what you put in and when, to monitor your expenses.

THE REWARDS OF TRAVEL

Being a savvy traveler isn't just a matter of practicality and organization. What we wish for every person who packs his or her bags to head off on a trip is a passion for travel. There is not much to compare with travel — it will give you more than you can possibly take from it. It will take you out of the comfort and complacency of all that is familiar; it will feed your senses and your intellect; it will heighten your understanding and compassion; and it will bestow upon you good friends and memories. Even the unfortunate travel episodes are not without their value — you are usually wiser for having gone through them!

CHAPTER TWO

RED TAPE

If you do not have a **valid passport,** apply for it a few months early. If you do have a passport, check to ensure that it will not expire until well after you plan to return home. If your passport will expire within two months of your return, apply for a renewal passport well in advance of your departure date.

U.S. passports are now **valid for ten years.** A brand new passport costs $35.00, plus a $7.00 processing fee levied by the local author ity executing your application. For information about where and how to apply for a passport locally, contact your local courthouse, town or county government, or post office.

The U.S. Department of State has **thirteen Passport Agency Offices,** located in Boston, Chicago, Honolulu, Houston, Los Angeles, Miami, New Orleans, New York, Philadelphia, San Francisco, Seattle, Stamford (Connecticut), and Washington, D.C., where you may apply in person and avoid the $7.00 processing fee. See Chapter 23, "Useful Addresses."

To apply for a passport, you will need: two identical, recent, 2-inch-square photos of yourself, full face, with a white background; a copy of your birth certificate bearing the seal of the issuing authority, or your Naturalization certificate if you are a naturalized citizen; and one additional piece of identification (such as a driver's license). You will be asked to repeat an oath.

If your passport is soon to expire, or expired less than three years ago, you may **apply by mail** to any of the Passport Agencies listed above. Obtain an "Application for Passport by Mail" (Form DPS-82) from your travel agent or a Passport Agency, complete the form, and send it to one of the Agencies along with your present passport, two recent passport-sized photographs signed on the reverse, and a check for $35.00, payable to "Passport Services."

If you ever applied for a **foreign passport,** or in any other way began the process of renouncing U.S. citizenship, you will have to explain that situation to passport officials. Allow extra time for this.

Keep your passport **on your person** at all times. Do not carry it in your suitcase, leave it on the airplane seat, or give it to another person who doesn't have a good reason for having it. Best of all is to carry it in a zippered pocket inside your clothes. Money belts are good; some travelers even carry their passport in a shoe!

You can **register your passport** at the U.S. Embassy upon your arrival in a foreign country. This greatly expedites the process if your passport is lost or stolen.

PASSPORT POINTERS

■ If you have changed your name, include with your application for renewal a copy of your marriage license or the certified court order verifying your name change. Otherwise the passport will be issued in the same name as the original.

■ Allow at least a month to get your new passport, and more time (three months is safest) if you're applying in the peak seasons, spring.

■ Apply in person, at any of the Passport Agencies listed above, if time is short. You can avoid some delays and explain any problems to the passport agent.

■ If passport officials know your departure date they will make an effort to get your passport to you on time.

■ In an emergency you can get a passport in one day. Apply in person with ticket or a letter from a travel agent at a passport office in the cities listed above.

■ A service that will obtain your passport for you (in one day, if necessary) is Passport Plus (800-367-1818). It is based in New York but operates nationwide.

If you do have to **get a passport overseas,** go to the American Embassy for a new one. The procedure will go much more smoothly if you have with you a copy of your birth certificate, an additional piece of identification such as a driver's license, and some extra passport-sized photographs. You will have to pay the full price of $35.00 for a new one, or in some cases, you may be issued a three-month temporary passport.

VISAS

Consult travel agents, airlines, consulates, or embassies about whether you need visas for the countries you are visiting. Different countries have different requirements, and many require foreign nationals to obtain, and show, visas before they can enter. (The United States requires visas for most foreign nationals.) A visa is simply an endorsement of your entry, and the granting of one indicates that your papers and your intended purpose (travel, work, study) are acceptable to that foreign government.

You **apply for a visa** in much the same way you apply for a passport. For most Westerners, obtaining a visa is simply a bureaucratic formality, because the governments involved are confident that we will be coming back to our own country.

Write directly to the **embassies or consulates** of the country or countries that you plan to visit for an application. Usually you will need a valid U.S. passport, a photograph, and a fee. Some countries require proof of vaccination, as well; others need to know your exact travel plans, how much money you will have with you, your address in the country, and how and when you'll be leaving. Frequently you must also declare that you have no intention of seeking employment in the country.

If time is short, or you are unsure about the application procedures, you can pay a **visa service** to do it for you. Your travel agent will have the addresses of visa services. They can be particularly helpful in obtaining difficult visas for countries to which Westerners rarely travel, or where there may be restrictions on the freedom of foreign visitors.

If you are **traveling on a train** that makes scheduled stops in other countries, you may well need a visa for those nations even if you do not get off the train. An official will board the train at the last stop before the border and ask to see passports and visas of all passengers. Your travel agent can look at the scheduled stops on your itinerary, and advise you on visa procedures.

Package tour operators often take care of visas for their customers, but you must double-check. It is your responsibility, ultimately.

DRIVING

If you plan to rent a car, you may obtain an **International Driving License** from your local automobile club. You do not need this license in any Western European country except Spain (your regular state driving license is sufficient); in Spain and many countries outside Western Europe you will need it. The license is valid for one year, requires two passport-sized photographs and a fee of $5.00, and is issued automatically if you present a valid state driver's license. When driving, always carry both your state license and your International Driving License.

TELEPHONES

Two things we take for granted in this country are our pure tap water and our telephone system. Although telephone technology is slowly infiltrating the most remote areas of the world, you will be surprised at the problems of foreign telephone systems even in highly industrialized countries.

Become familiar with the **pay phone** in the country you're visiting, both for convenience and safety. Many pay phones do not accept money until the connection is made; if you put a coin in when you pick up the receiver, you lose it. Often you will dial the number, and when it is answered there will be a loud buzz until you insert the correct coins.

In other countries there are public telephones known as **"tax-iphones,"** because they calculate the cost of your call based on how long you talk and at what distance you're calling. Such phones require tokens; be sure to have a good supply at hand.

Avoid calling **from your hotel room;** there's always an exorbitant fee (sometimes double or triple the cost) added to your bill for this service.

The best bet for an **international call** is to call from an International Telephone and Telegraph Office, often located in the post office. Use your telephone credit card, if you have one. You will give the number you wish to call to the clerk, who will put through the call and assign you to a booth. You pay when you're finished.

In more and more foreign countries, you can now **dial international calls directly** from a pay phone. It's most convenient if you use a credit card or call collect.

Use **the telephone book** in a foreign country; it will often have a page in English that can give you the number to dial for a multilingual operator.

MAIL

"Poste Restante" or General Delivery at the Main Post Office of the city is always reliable for receiving mail. You will need your passport. Note that post offices often close for the midday meal in foreign countries, and that the "Poste Restante" window may have even shorter hours than the main window. The post office will keep a letter for 30 days before returning it to the sender.

If there is an American Express office in the country you are visiting, that is an excellent place to receive mail (and meet your fellow travelers!), as long as you have American Express traveler's checks or a credit card.

If you're not the type who buys souvenirs, try instead **writing postcards to yourself.** That way you'll have a postcard of a favorite place or monument, and some postage stamps, as a special remembrance upon your return.

If you are mailing a letter in some Third World countries, be sure to take it to the post office and **watch the clerk cancel the stamp.** Uncancelled stamps can be stolen off letters, especially in places where the cost of one stamp can buy a full meal.

CHAPTER THREE

MONEY

On a recent two-week trip to Switzerland, a friend of ours watched with consternation as the dollar took a slow downward slide. Ten dollars bought her sixteen and a half Swiss francs when she arrived, and only fifteen by the time she left. How can you protect yourself against this kind of exchange-rate erosion?

When budgeting for your trip, imagine the worst, money-wise — that the U.S. dollar suddenly starts losing value against all major foreign currencies. Prepare for things to cost even more than you expect. If you allow for a twenty percent increase in costs you will be protected — and you will be pleasantly surprised if the dollar gains, rather than declines, during your trip!

Sometimes the exchange rate may actually **dictate where you go.** If Venezuela is giving a good rate on the dollar you might decide to go there instead of to the Bahamas.

It's helpful to **establish priorities** for your budget. On some trips, we decided that eating well was our priority — that we would save on lodgings but splurge on the local cuisine. (In the tropics, for example, you might choose to eat in more expensive restaurants to be sure of adequate sanitation.) Other places, lodging was paramount — we wanted to be right on the beach, or downtown in a city. You may wish to focus on entertainment — you're in London and you're willing to save on meals and lodging in order to attend the theatre every night. Even if you can't splurge on anything on your trip, it's helpful to have set spending priorities like this.

Don't wait till the **day before departure** to purchase traveler's checks! There might be a snowstorm, or a holiday you didn't bank on.

Take with you about **fifty U.S. dollars** in small bills for last-minute emergencies and for getting home again.

Try to obtain, in advance, **fifty to one hundred dollars in the currency** of your destination. You won't get a good rate of exchange, but you won't have to worry about finding a bank and coping with long lines immediately upon arrival. Order your foreign currency at least a month ahead of time through your bank (the yen, for instance, can be hard to buy in the United States).

If the dollar is sinking as you are making your trip preparations, and you believe it will continue to do so, you may wish to purchase **traveler's checks in the currency of your destination,** to "fix" an exchange rate. This is always a gamble, however — the dollar may suddenly start rising again.

Having your money in traveler's checks is obviously safest. Another advantage is that traveler's checks often receive a **better exchange rate** than cash does.

Some travelers like to purchase a lot of **small-denomination traveler's checks,** so they won't be carrying around a lot of cash. Others prefer to buy denominations no smaller than $50, so that they're not constantly cashing checks. We happen to be in the latter group. We have found that some exchange places charge a set service fee per transaction, so that it is expensive to keep exchanging small amounts of money.

Before leaving home, **make a list of the numbers** of all your traveler's checks, and add the city and date purchased (see Chapter 22 for a Safety Numbers List). Give a copy of this list to a friend or relative at home, and take a copy along with you in a sealed envelope in your suitcase.

Local banks and American Express or Thomas Cook, Ltd. offices usually give the **best exchange rates.** Avoid changing money at your hotel or in shops; an exorbitant fee is usually added. However, there are exceptions in different countries, and you will have to rely on guidebooks or on other travelers for advice. In Brazil, for example, hotels can have the best exchange rate, while in Switzerland, train stations may be best. In Communist countries, the rate of exchange is set by the government, and so it's the same everywhere.

Banks in other countries tend to have **fewer hours** than they do in the United States. Many banks close for an hour or two at noon. Be sure to learn the bank schedules in the country you're visiting.

The bank will post a sign listing the **exchange rates for the day.** Under "U.S. $" there will be two columns, one headed "Buy" and one headed "Sell." If you are in England, it might say £1.20 under "Buy" and £1.25 under "Sell." You are concerned with the "Buy" column, because the bank is buying your dollars. In this case, you would get £12.00 for $10.00. The "Sell" figure is always higher than the "Buy" figure.

You will **need your passport** in order to cash traveler's checks. At some American Express offices, your traveler's checks must be American Express.

Once you have obtained some foreign money, **take a good look at it.** Examine the coins and figure out how to tell them apart. Look at the bills. You want to be familiar enough with them so that you will be as quick as possible in your monetary transactions. Travelers often end up with pockets or purses bulging with change, because they are constantly breaking large bills. And change does not usually convert back to U.S. currency.

Bring along a **pocket calculator** to figure the exchange rate if you'll be doing serious shopping.

But **don't get hung up** on your exchange rate. It changes from day to day and is impossible to predict. You can ruin your trip by fretting about the better rate available around the corner from where you cashed your check.

Save the receipts of all the money you change. Many countries require that when you leave you show these receipts if you want to convert local currency back to dollars (to ensure that you aren't making money off the black market).

Keep the record of your traveler's checks **separate** from the checks themselves. If you carry the checks in your purse or money belt, keep the record in your suitcase. It's much harder to be reimbursed without this record.

Since your record is separate from your checks, you'll be unable to write down exactly when you cash each check. Instead, **update your record** every evening. You don't need to remember where you cashed your checks — the important thing is to list the numbers of those you cashed, so that you have an accurate record of those remaining uncashed, in case they are stolen. Keep the receipt from each transaction with the record.

If your traveler's checks are lost or stolen, contact the nearest branch office of the issuing company and report the loss. You may be reimbursed right away. Have your passport with you.

If you do not have the record of numbers of checks lost (those remaining uncashed on your list), you will have to **telephone or wire your own bank,** where you purchased the checks, or the friend or relative with whom you left a copy of the list.

CREDIT CARDS

Credit cards are a tremendous convenience on a trip. Not only do they allow you to postpone payment for transportation, lodgings, purchases, etc., but many can also help you to obtain cash in an emergency. If you use your credit card to shop, you'll have a receipt at the time of the transaction, a monthly statement, and a period of financial float before you must pay.

On the other hand, it is very easy to exceed your budget by overspending on credit cards. If you wish to monitor your expenses, it might be wise to limit credit card use to particular types of expenses, such as emergencies and travel accommodations (transportation, hotels, meals).

Any foreign purchase made with a credit card will be converted to dollars for billing purposes, and many times the credit card companies will make that conversion at an inflated rate of exchange. You will be billed according to the rate of exchange **effective on the day**

your charge clears in the United States, not on the day you made the purchase.

Credit cards are often accepted at hotels and good restaurants. Aside from these two instances, the **acceptance of credit cards can vary** from country to country. Some shops won't take them because they have to pay the credit card company a percentage of their total sale.

Visa is the most widely accepted and used credit card in the world. **American Express,** on the other hand, offers you the broadest range of travel services. With the **MasterCard Gold** you have a minimum credit line of $5,000 and many travel, insurance, shopping and emergency-cash services.

Leave at home any credit cards that will not be useful where you are going. Those you do take should be carefully guarded. **Make a list** of their serial numbers and the company's emergency phone numbers (see Chapter 22, "Safety Numbers List") before you leave home. Give a copy to a friend at home along with your itinerary and the list of your traveler's check numbers, and take a copy along with you.

If you use an American Express Card to buy plane, boat, or train tickets, you will be **automatically insured** for $100,000 worth of travel accident insurance and $1,000 of baggage insurance.

When you charge something, **examine the charge slip** carefully and keep your customer copy so that you can compare it to your final bill.

With most credit cards (including American Express, Master-Card Gold, Visa, and Diners Club International) you can **obtain cash abroad.** Check with the company for information. American Express Cardmembers can cash personal checks from $50 to $150 by showing their card at selected hotels and airline ticket counters. In an American Express travel agency you can cash a bigger check and get part in cash and most in traveler's checks. Holders of the Sears Discover card or Diners Club card can cash modest personal checks at any Sears store or Citibank branch office, respectively.

ATM Systems

Many banks now belong to large national and international ATM (automatic teller machine) systems that allow you to get cash at all hours of the day or night and have it deducted from your checking account or charged to your credit card. Ask about this service at your bank or call the toll-free customer service number on your credit card bill. Remember these features of the ATM service:

You may be charged a small fee for each transaction in which you request cash at an ATM machine.

There is a dollar limit to how much you can withdraw daily using your ATM card.

When you use your ATM card to obtain cash overseas, you will receive the local currency, not dollars. And you will be billed according to the rate of exchange on the day the charge clears in the U.S., not the rate in effect on the day of the transaction.

Miscellaneous

If you'll be in only one or two foreign countries, try to **think in the currency** of the place, rather than constantly converting it to dollars. Not only will this save you time whenever you're making a purchase — especially when you're bargaining a price down! — but it will also help you understand the country's economics a little better. Ten rupees may be equivalent to a dollar, which seems very little to an American, but it may be the average day's wage in the country you're visiting.

This brings us to the issue of **beggars.** Being approached by beggars, whether they are a gang of adorable street urchins, a mother with a crying baby, or a paraplegic on a temple's steps, is a wrenching experience, and a challenge to your heart and your conscience. This is one of those situations where there can be no hard and fast rule. Remember, however, that you will be approached again and again in some countries, whether you have given money or not. If you give some coins to a mother with a baby, you may help her out for one day, but she will be in need again tomorrow. And you could give all of your money to beggars and not solve a miniscule part of that country's problems. In general, we don't give money to beggars, but we do make exceptions. And we certainly would reward someone who performed a service for us — such as carrying our bags or watching our car.

CHAPTER FOUR

HEALTH

For addresses of organizations listing reliable, English-speaking, overseas physicians, see Chapter 23, "Useful Addresses."

There's a joke that says the only thing you really need in order to enjoy travel is a strong stomach. We would add "and some common sense." Certainly the most important priority in traveling is to stay healthy; one of the most miserable experiences imaginable is to get sick when you're far from home.

We've heard that one-third of all international travelers suffer from diarrhea on their trip, and half of those going to certain countries with poor sanitation. So what do the others do right? Some people are blessed with a robust digestive system to begin with; others simply take great care to stay out of trouble. (See "Diarrhea," below).

Schedule an **appointment with your doctor** for about four to six weeks before your departure date. You will need:

A basic physical exam

A schedule of immunizations

An updating of any prescriptions you require — enough to last the trip

Your **physical exam** should include routine blood tests, a review of your medical records, and any necessary booster shots (tetanus, polio, etc.).

Have your physician write out the **generic or scientific name** of any drug prescribed so that foreign pharmacists won't be confused by brand names.

19

Your physician may also be able to prescribe medicines to protect you against **overexposure to the sun, diarrhea, and motion sickness.**

Make sure you have copies of your prescriptions for **contact lenses and glasses** as well.

Any essential drugs and prescriptions should be carried **on board the airplane** with you, not checked in your luggage.

Older travelers in particular may wish to ask their doctor to fill out a sheet on their **medical background,** including blood type, drug allergies, special conditions, and any pertinent medical history. Have the physician include his or her address.

We recommend having a **dental checkup,** too. One of us once tried to explore Dublin while suffering from a toothache, and it was a most unhappy day. Obtaining dental care in a foreign country is a risky business. Have your teeth cleaned and X-rayed and your fillings checked for secure fit.

If you have a medical condition that should be known about in an emergency (diabetes, epilepsy, heart condition, pregnancy), obtain a **Medic Alert bracelet** from Medic Alert Foundation, P.O. Box 1009, Turlock, CA 95381 or 777 U.N. Plaza, New York, NY 10017.

IMMUNIZATIONS

Some immunizations may be required before you can visit certain countries; others are not required but are strongly recommended to protect your health. If your physician does not know which ones you need, you can contact the Center for Disease Control in Atlanta (see Chapter 23, "Useful Addresses").

At the passport agency or Public Health agency, obtain the "International Certificate of Vaccination" (often referred to as your yellow card), on which your inoculations will be recorded. This is required before entering some countries, and you will find it a valuable life-long record. Keep it with your passport.

Pregnant women should generally avoid vaccinations unless absolutely necessary.

Note that you may be able to get inoculations for free at the U.S. Public Health Department.

You may need:

■ Immunizations for cholera, yellow fever, and typhoid

■ Anti-malaria pills to take during the trip and for two months after your return

■ An injection of gamma globulin to lower risk of Hepatitis A

■ Immunizations or boosters to protect you against other common diseases

At this writing, only cholera and yellow fever shots are mandatory before going to certain areas of the world. Typhoid shots may be recommended as well, if you are going to less developed parts of South America, Africa, and Asia.

Yellow Fever. Some countries require proof of yellow fever vaccination before visas are issued or entry is permitted. Yellow fever certificates are good for ten years. It is recommended that you get this vaccination if you are going to any country that has yellow fever.

Cholera. The risk of cholera for American travelers is very low, and the vaccine is considered relatively ineffective. Generally, if you avoid unsafe food and water, your chance of contracting cholera is extremely slight. A few countries still require proof of cholera vaccination The vaccine is administered twice, a week apart, and is good for six months. If you are pregnant, you should not be vaccinated.

Typhoid. If you are traveling to Central America, South America, or Asia, and especially if you will visit remote rural areas, a typhoid vaccination is strongly recommended (but not required). Plan to get the first shot a month before departure. The vaccine is administered twice, four weeks apart, and is good for two years.

Gamma Globulin. This injection will help protect you against Hepatitis A and should be taken if you are going to areas with poor sanitation. It is most effective immediately after administered, and it is effective for three to six months. If you get a booster during your trip, make sure the hospital or clinic has excellent sanitary standards.

Malaria. There is no approved vaccine for malaria, as yet. The disease is carried by mosquitoes, and is present in more than 100 countries, especially in the rural areas in Mexico, Central America, South America, Africa, the Middle East, Asia (including India and Southeast Asia), and Oceania. If you travel to any of these areas, you will be at risk, and you should protect yourself. Your doctor will prescribe a weekly dose of anti-malarial medication (usually chloroquine), starting at least two weeks before you enter malaria territory and ending six weeks after you return home.

In some areas of the world, the malaria parasite is resistant to chloroquine, and you will need to take an additional medicine called Fansidar. Ask your doctor if you need this.

If you are taking Fansidar, and you come down with a rash, you may be experiencing a reaction to the drug. Discontinue it.

Symptoms of malaria include fever with chills and headache. Do not interpret this as the flu — demand medical attention as soon as possible. Malaria can be cured if discovered early.

Measles. Wherever you are going, it is wise to make sure you're immune to this serious disease. If you were born before 1957, you are probably naturally immune through having contracted it in childhood.

Tetanus. No matter where you are going, you should have the primary series (two shots, four weeks apart) if you were never vaccinated, and a booster shot every ten years.

Meningcoccal. Call your state Department of Health to find out whether the areas you are visiting have current epidemics of this disease.

Polio. There are still areas of the world (tropical regions and developing countries) where polio is a threat. Contact your state Department of Health.

Smallpox. This disease is no longer a threat — a victory for medicine. You no longer need a smallpox shot to enter any country.

If you are staying **on the beaten path,** or if you are merely visiting a city on business, your chances of contracting a serious disease are much less than with the traveler who likes to explore remote areas.

WATER

Water, which we in North America take so much for granted, may in other parts of the world be heavily contaminated by disease-causing organisms.

Generally, the water in Canada, Northern Europe, Australia, New Zealand, and the United States is of excellent quality — sometimes even famous for its purity. If the water where you are is not known to be up to these standards, however, you should drink only the following:

- Water that has been boiled or treated (see below)
- Beverages such as coffee and tea made with boiled water
- Canned or bottled carbonated water and soft drinks
- Beer and wine

Anytime you take a trip your system may need time to adjust to the drinking water, even if you're still in the United States. If you are flying from the West Coast to the East Coast, for example, it's wise to drink no more than one glass of water the first day of your trip.

In major European cities, tap water is generally excellent. The exceptions may be Italy, Spain, Portugal, and Greece — although traveler's experiences vary. If you are in doubt, purchase one of the many different brands of bottled water and have it with you in your hotel room.

TREATING WATER

Boiling is the most reliable way to make water safe. If you cannot boil the water, treatment with iodine or halazone tablets is an acceptable alternative. Chlorine may be used, but is slightly less reliable than iodine.

To treat water by boiling, let it boil vigorously for five minutes. Allow it to cool, covered, to room temperature. Do not add ice. If you are at a very high altitude, boil the water for ten minutes, or chemically disinfect after boiling.

To treat water chemically, add 5 drops tincture of iodine per quart or liter of clear water, or 10 drops per quart or liter if the water is cloudy or very cold. Allow the water to stand for 30 minutes after drops have been added before drinking. If the water is cloudy or very cold, let the water stand from 60 to 90 minutes.

Halazone tablets, available from pharmacies and sporting goods stores, are also acceptable. Follow the manufacturer's instructions. If the water is cloudy or very cold, double the number of tablets and the standing time.

Other tips:

■ If the water you are using cannot be boiled, strain it through a clean cloth to remove sediment, and then treat it with iodine or tablets.

■ You may use an immersible heater coil to boil the water (if the voltage is appropriate).

■ If the water is contaminated, ice will be, too. Use ice made only from boiled water.

■ If a container has held unsafe water, it will contaminate fresh water poured into it. Be sure to clean all containers thoroughly before using them.

■ Boil or treat unsafe water before brushing your teeth with it.

■ Do not drink bottled non-carbonated water where there is inadequate sanitation, even if it is advertised as mineral water.

■ If the water tastes bad, add a pinch of salt.

■ Even the moisture that condenses on the outside of a can or bottle may be contaminated. Wipe off any moisture that has accumulated where your mouth will touch the container. Better still, use a drinking straw.

If you will be living in a major city in a foreign country, where the tap water is of good quality, **you may be able to adjust** to drinking it if you go slowly. Treat the water before even brushing your teeth, at first. Then use untreated water for brushing teeth and notice your reaction — if you experience any diarrhea, continue treating all water. If you had no ill reactions, continue boiling drinking water for shorter and shorter periods. Eventually you may be able to drink it straight.

MILK

In many countries milk is as good as or superior to that in the United States. These are the countries where the government controls and regulates every stage of milk production — Great Britain, Ireland, Scandinavia, West Germany, the Netherlands, Switzerland, and many more.

In places where the milk is not of good quality, you must avoid ice cream and soft cheeses as well. If you are uncertain of the quality of the milk, boil it before drinking it.

FOOD

Enjoying the native cuisine and the local delicacies can be one of the greatest pleasures of traveling. If you are in an area where sanitation is poor, however, be very selective about what you eat. There are exceptions to most of the following tips; use them only as guidelines. If you learn to know your own constitution you'll know how well you can handle strange foods.

FOODS TO AVOID IN THE TROPICS

■ Raw fruits — unless they can be peeled and you do the peeling. Stick to those fruits that have natural protection in their peels, such as oranges, pineapples, and bananas (you will find that bananas come in many varieties in tropical countries and are a true delicacy).

■ Raw vegetables — especially lettuce and salads. Well-cooked vegetables are usually safe.

■ Raw or rare meat or fish.

Eat well-cooked foods that are still hot. Avoid anything that has been cooked and has stood a while.

A common warning is to avoid food purchased from street vendors. This is a good rule of thumb, but **consult other travelers** you meet. You might not want to miss the fresh juices of Mexico, the delicious broiled beef at stalls along the streets of Bolivia, or the famous night market, with food stalls, in Penang, Malaysia. Again, know your own metabolism. If you do not tend to have digestive problems, try some samples; if you do, don't take a chance.

DIARRHEA

There are precautions you can take against diarrhea without having to lessen the pleasures of your trip. Don't even brush your teeth with untreated water in places where sanitation is poor. Wash your hands before eating and after using the toilet. Eat only well-cooked foods, or fruits and vegetables that you peel yourself. Learn to quench your thirst with tea, coffee, bottled soda, and bottled carbonated water.

A bout of diarrhea ("turista," "Delhi belly," or "Montezuma's revenge") is usually **over in three or four days.** Go to a doctor if it persists for more than five days, if you see blood in your stool, if you experience fever or chills, or if you become dehydrated.

Do not take **Enterovioform** for diarrhea.

Our advice is to hole up for a few days in a **clean hotel room** that has a clean bathroom, either attached or easily accessible, with a lock on the door. Here are some more tips to ease your misery:

■ Remember to drink plenty of fluids to prevent dehydration — a dangerous complication of diarrhea, especially for children. Dehydration is marked by excessive thirst and weakness in adults, and by listlessness and dry mouth in infants. Children in particular must be encouraged to drink a lot of clear liquids, such as bottled carbonated water. Add a pinch of salt and a pinch of sugar. Colas are fine.

■ If you use **Lomotil,** use it only for one or two days. It will stop the diarrhea, but it will also prevent you from getting rid of the germs.

■ Avoid cow's milk until recovery.

■ Cut down on coffee consumption.

■ Reduce your intake of solids. Eat bland foods — soft-boiled eggs, rice, potatoes, macaroni, crackers, bread — until you recover. In India ask for a dish called kedgeree, famous for restoring the health.

■ If your child becomes sick with diarrhea, be especially vigilant in administering the fluids. Dehydration comes on more quickly with children, and is a very serious problem. Contact a doctor if your child with diarrhea becomes feverish or appears ill.

CONSTIPATION

Many travelers, especially older ones, complain of the opposite problem — constipation. Laxatives are not the best answer because the body quickly can become dependent on them.

The best way to avoid constipation is to eat **a healthy diet.** Make sure you are getting fiber from different sources — bran cereals, fruits, vegetables, beans, and whole-grain breads.

Also important is to get **plenty of exercise,** which seems to have a laxative effect on the body. Walking is best, and will be good for

The **World Health Organization** has come up with the following formula to replenish fluids lost during diarrhea. Prepare two separate glasses of the following:

Glass 1
8 oz. water (boiled or carbonated)
1 T. honey, corn syrup, or table sugar
¼ t. table salt

Glass 2
8 oz. orange, lemon, or coconut juice or 8 oz. water if fruit juice is un-
   available
¼ t. baking soda

Drink alternately from each glass. Infants should continue to breastfeed or receive plain (treated) water as desired while receiving these solutions.

If the above ingredients are unobtainable, drink liberally of a variety of safe liquids, including treated water, canned fruit juices, hot tea with sugar, and carbonated drinks. Or take 2 T. honey and 2 T. vinegar or salt in a glass of warm water, to replace fluids and minerals lost.

your health generally. Activities that tone the muscles of the abdomen — bicycling, yoga, and swimming — are also beneficial.

ON THE ROAD

The leading hazard for travelers in a foreign country is automobile accidents, undoubtedly because of unfamiliarity with foreign traffic laws. (See also Chapter 9, "Getting Around.")

Be sure to familiarize yourself with **international road signs** before you get behind the steering wheel in a strange country.

Make sure to **wear your seat belt** — do not rent a car that doesn't have them.

The same goes with **infant car seats.** If necessary, invest in the kind of car seat that can double as an infant's airplane seat. Hertz cars will supply infant car seats in Europe, but you must return them to the city of origin.

Make sure you have recovered from jet lag before you drive.

To prevent **car sickness,** make sure no one smokes in the car. Eat a hearty breakfast before the trip and eat light snacks on the road. Avoid alcohol, and do not drink tea on an empty stomach.

PERSONAL HYGIENE

If you are traveling outside the United States, you will quickly discover that in most of the world the daily shower is an undreamt-of luxury. Water, and especially heated water, are simply not that plentiful. Our advice is to adapt as much as possible to what you find — whether it's a waterfall to bathe in on a beach in Mexico or that marvelous French invention, a bidet. In the tropics, rainwater is saved and carefully portioned out, yet you will find your hosts anticipate your needs and might go without a cup of tea themselves so that you can wash your face. If you can learn to be satisfied with a daily sponge bath instead of a shower, you will be most comfortable.

Bathing your feet at the end of a long day can be almost as restorative as a hot shower. Bring along some Pickle's Foot Cream, available from Caswell-Massey, Mail Order Division, 111 Eighth Avenue, New York, NY 10011.

Bring also any **health aids** you find indispensable. We always bring dental floss, which often greatly amuses our hosts. Women will find that tampons are often available only in big cities.

If you're traveling in your own car, camper, or boat, the American Red Cross has designed the perfect **first-aid kit** for you. Resembling

FIRST-AID KIT

A small first-aid kit should include the following:

bandages	tweezer
analgesics (aspirin or	fingernail clipper
acetaminophen)	foil-wrapped sterile wipes
thermometer	antibiotic cream
sunscreen	multiple vitamins
nasal decongestant	foot cream or powder

Other useful items to bring, depending on where and how you are traveling, could include:

insect repellent containing N,N diethyl metatoluamide (deet)
oil of cloves for toothache
water purifier — iodine drops or halazone tablets
calamine lotion (for insect bites, poison ivy, and sunburn)

a vinyl, foam-padded pillow, 10"x12", it unzips to reveal clearly labeled pockets containing bandages and sterile wipes, a waterproof blanket, a triangular bandage, and scissors. The sale of this kit supports the Red Cross. Write American Red Cross Automobile First-Aid Kit, Box D, Haworth, NJ 07641.

Sexually Transmitted Diseases

Men and women who intend to have romantic adventures while traveling should be certain to bring their own supply of condoms. Do not expect your partner to be equipped.

Insects

If you're traveling in the tropics, you will certainly notice the insects — they seem to be three times as big as they are here. Malaria is only one of the diseases that are carried by insects. If you follow the recommended regime of malaria prophylaxis, you will probably be safe from that disease, but you may wish to take other precautions as well in tropical countries:

■ Use mosquito netting over beds and infants' cribs.

■ Use insect repellents containing N,N. diethyl metatoluamide (deet).

■ Mosquito coils, which are available in other countries, are effective.

■ Wear long sleeves and long pants, in light colors.

■ Be sure to be protected at dusk, mosquitoes' favorite time.

To **extract a tick** safely from the skin, cover it with olive oil, mineral oil, petroleum jelly, or nail polish, any of which will force it to withdraw its head to avoid suffocating. Pluck it out with a tweezer, and disinfect the area.

Bees do not carry diseases, but a few people are extremely allergic. A severe reaction can lead to death, if left untreated, so this must be treated as a medical emergency. Find medical assistance immediately. In the meantime, scrape the stinger out with a knife blade or fingernail (do not try to pull it out).

The normal reaction to a bee sting is pain, swelling, and itching. Relieve these with calamine lotion, an ice pack and an analgesic.

In this country, **swimming in freshwater ponds** and streams is usually (but not always) safe. In many parts of the world, however, you can emerge with one of a number of skin, eye, ear, or intestinal infections. Well-chlorinated swimming pools and the ocean are your best bets.

SUNBURN

Remember that the tropical sun can inflict a wretched burn on tender, winter-pale skin. If you are in a hurry to get a tan, you may instead get the burn of your life, which can be temporarily crippling. Take these precautions:

■ Restrict your first day's sunbathing in the tropics to ten minutes, the second to fifteen, and the third to twenty.

■ Use a good sunscreen, and reapply after swimming or showering.

■ Wear a hat and long sleeves at other times.

■ Stay out of the hottest sun, from noon to three p.m.

■ If you do get burned anyway, use calamine lotion, vinegar, or the gel of the aloe vera plant to soothe the skin.

■ Drink fresh fruit juices, or water with a squeeze of fresh lemon or lime juice.

SKIING

Dazzling sun on snow can cause a severe sunburn, too. Make sure you wear sunglasses, a good sunscreen, and, if your skin is tender, zinc oxide on lips and nose.

One of us once sprained an ankle skiing in Montana's high country the morning after a grueling night flight. If you're on a ski vacation, give yourself time to **recover from jet lag** and adjust to the altitude, especially if you are out of shape. Otherwise your judgment and reflexes may not be up to par. Take it easy for the first few days — get a good night's sleep and take a break every few hours during the day.

IF YOU GET SICK OR HURT

Contact the American consulate or embassy (or the Canadian, British, Irish, or Australian consulate) to find the name of a reliable English-speaking physician.

American hospitals, large government-run hospitals, or missionary clinics are likely to have good physicians.

If you need a **prescription filled** after hours in Europe, every pharmacy will have on its door a sign listing the name and address of the pharmacy that is open that night.

You may encounter overseas certain drugs that you should be careful of. **Aminopyrine,** which is sold as an analgesic in Japan, is very unsafe for people of Anglo-Saxon descent. **Enterovioform** has serious side effects and is considered of questionable value in treating traveler's diarrhea.

Although many European countries will give you health care for free under their public health systems, some will charge a high **fee before admitting you** to a hospital. Emergency assistance plans (see below) will come through for you in this situation.

Major hospitals in large cities or American-owned hospitals may accept **credit cards** for service.

INSURANCE

Check with your insurance company well in advance of your trip to make sure you will be covered wherever you go. Some policies, such as Medicare, have geographic restrictions. Other policies may not cover 100 percent of your costs incurred outside the U.S.

In addition to any special insurance you've acquired for your trip, you should be certain that your normal medical and health insurance is up to date.

Carry your insurance card, your agent's telephone number and address, and your insurance company's telephone number. Bring along an insurance claim form so that it can be filled out by the physician that treats you. Some companies, such as Blue Cross and Blue Shield, will not reimburse you unless such a form has been properly filled out.

A form of insurance that is especially useful for travelers is the **emergency assistance plan.**

An assistance plan will give you money on the spot to help you through an emergency. It may also have a 24-hour operator whom you can call collect to get immediate help. Teams of multilingual emergency assistance professionals will help you deal with any crisis from getting a prescription filled in the middle of the night to getting evacuated after an accident. They can help you find a physician, dentist, or medical facility; they may wire you money for hospital admission; they will pay your hospital and medical expenses up to $5,000 or more; they will contact your own physician in order to monitor the care you are receiving; they will arrange for you to be moved to a different hospital or back home. (See Chapter 23, "Useful Address," for names of companies.)

If you're going on a European skiing vacation, you can purchase a **Carte Neige** (literally, "Snow Card"), available through French travel agencies, which will provide emergency assistance and evacuation if you have a ski accident.

If you are an **American Express Cardmember** you automatically get accident coverage on a common carrier (plane, ship, train, or bus), if you charged your trip.

Some insurance plans offer **coverage for one year,** not just for a single trip. This is directed primarily at the business traveler, and usually requires that you not be outside of the country for more than 90 days at a time.

Many policies have an **age limit,** usually 70. If you are a Medicare patient and would like supplemental coverage for a trip out of the country, contact the American Association of Retired Persons (See Chapter 23, "Useful Addresses").

Some policies limit coverage of accidents involving **active sports** such as skiing or scuba diving, unless you pay an extra fee.

Third-trimester pregnant women are often excluded from coverage.

In countries to which the U.S. government discourages travel, such as (at this writing) Afghanistan, Burma, El Salvador, Iran, Iraq, Kampuchea, Laos, Lebanon, Nicaragua, North Korea, South Yemen, and Vietnam, you may not be covered.

If you have a serious medical emergency, the Overseas Citizens' Emergency Center, under the U.S. State Department, may be able to help out. They will notify your relatives of your problems, help transmit funds to you, and expedite the sending of medical information back and forth. See Chapter 23, "Useful Addresses."

CHAPTER FIVE

WHAT TO TAKE

The wisest travel advice we've heard is to bring half the clothes and twice the money. Packing light is the first law of carefree travel. Yet it can be difficult, when you're actually packing, to leave behind that special sweater, those dressy clothes, that extra jacket ... "just in case." It's as if you want to take a little bit of home along with you for security. Before you know it you've got an unbelievably heavy, bulging, unwieldy bag.

Once on your trip, the weight of your bag becomes much more of a concern to you than the actual items you have brought. Rushing to catch a train, walking an extra mile to your hotel because you couldn't find a bus, constantly counting your bags to make sure you have everything — these are just a few of the times you will curse the extras and wish you had been more disciplined.

Not only will you be less exhausted if you pack light, but you will also be much more flexible, mobile, and spontaneous. One of us has a particularly fond memory of walking across a South Indian mountain range for a day, instead of having to take a grueling three-day bus trip the long way around — an option only possible because her luggage was just a small rucksack.

If you're going to stay in one place, or if you're going on a cruise, you will of course be able to bring more clothes. If you will be moving around a lot, you'll be painfully aware of the unneeded things in your bag.

Here are some tips to help you streamline.

WHAT TO BRING

Don't buy a **new wardrobe** before you go. (Save that money for your trip!) It's very annoying to drag around clothes that you don't like after all. Bring your favorite clothes — familiar, comfortable things that you know look good on you. After all, everything you wear will be new to the people you'll be seeing.

The most important items in your luggage, we believe, are **your shoes.** Make sure they are sturdy, with non-slip soles, and well broken in ahead of time. Have a cobbler replace heels and insert arch supports, if necessary. Give them a treatment with mink oil or other waterproofer. Bring along some lambswool or bandages to prevent blisters if you'll be walking a lot.

Even your **dress shoes** should be familiar and comfortable. You never know when you might find yourself on a romantic moonlit stroll along the Seine — an experience that would be ruined by blisters or sore feet.

The only items we do recommend purchasing just before you leave are **undergarments and socks,** which can be hard to obtain on a trip. (These will give the same psychological uplift as if you had bought all new clothes anyway!)

If you are traveling with another person, aim to go light enough so that **each of you can carry all the luggage** if necessary. This will be helpful, for example, if you have to have to find seats on a crowded train. One of you can go ahead and find the seats while the other follows with the bags.

Don't pack an **article you rarely wear,** thinking you might be in the mood to wear it. It will surely stay at the bottom of your suitcase the entire trip.

In some Third World countries, even the cheapest hotel will have a laundry service that comes to your door and picks up and delivers your things. These services are inexpensive and generally reliable, and the clothes will return after quite an adventure — being pounded on river rocks, baked in the sun, and given a knife-edge pressing. (Cot-

tons respond well to this treatment; delicate items and knits do not.)
Make a list of every item sent out.

Do not bring expensive clothes that require **dry cleaning,**
unless you are very confident that the service will be good. Bring things
you can wash yourself, either by hand or at a laundromat, or that you
can entrust without too much concern to a launderer.

Choose your clothes for their **lightness and washability.** You
want things that will stay wrinkle-free, wash easily, and take up a tiny
amount of space.

Choose your clothes around **one main coordinating color.** Make
sure each of your pants or skirts can be worn with each of your shirts or
blouses.

Scarves, belts, and costume jewelry, which don't take up much
room, can change the look of an outfit from day to day or from day to
evening.

You may notice that women in other countries **dress up more**
than they do in the United States, especially for dinner in a restaurant.
Although pants are acceptable dress for women today the world over,
you may want to bring along at least one skirt if you expect to be eating
frequently in restaurants. Dressing with dignity is the key in a foreign
culture.

Unless you're expecting to dine with royalty, leave your **expensive jewelry** at home — in the safety deposit box! It will only be a worry
on your trip.

We recommend **sewing inner pockets** to your clothes, and
adding buttons, snaps, or Velcro tape to existing pockets. Back pockets
of pants are especially vulnerable to pickpockets. Loose bills and change
are safer in your front pants pocket than in a handbag. Women may
want to add pockets to clothes that lack them.

In many foreign countries, you will not find special brands of
toiletries you or your family prefer. Any toilet items you consider essential should be **purchased in advance** and brought along.

A **sewing kit** can be handy. Include several large-eyed needles, thread that matches the colors of your clothes, extra buttons, and plenty of safety pins. A fingernail clipper can serve as scissors. In Europe you can buy a braid of thread of all different colors — when you need a certain color, you just pluck a thread from the braid.

Pick up a **city or country map** of your destination before you go, and become familiar with it. Find out where your hotel is and circle it on the map.

If you'll be encountering **different temperature extremes,** plan to layer your clothes. A turtleneck-shirt-sweater-shell combination will be warm enough for most climates. The shirt alone will suit warmer weather, and the shell will be enough for a cool evening.

Similarly, **if you're hiking,** plan to dress in layers. A turtleneck, flannel shirt, and nylon windbreaker will be just as effective, more versatile, and much less bulky than a sweater.

Bring plenty of **cotton or wool socks** if you expect to be doing a lot of walking.

If you're **traveling in winter,** determine where you'll be spending your time. If outdoors, you'll need a warm coat, but if you're attending a seminar or otherwise planning to be indoors most of the time, you might get by with a raincoat and a warm sweater.

Business travelers must take more clothes than recreational travelers, since they must make an immaculate impression. A spilled cup of coffee can ruin the deal and the trip if you don't have a complete change of clothing. See Chapter 21, "The Business Traveler."

Remember that you can purchase, at your destination, **clothes that fit the climate** and the ambience. The silks of Asia and the cottons of the tropics are lovely and inexpensive. You can have clothes made for you in Asia. Woolens, on the other hand, are great buys in Northern Europe, South America, Australia and New Zealand. (Occasionally, though, items purchased abroad may become just souvenirs of your trip, rarely if ever worn again — the daring bikini from the French Riviera, or the Indian sari.)

Things the streamlined traveler can do without: pajamas and nightgowns (a T-shirt will do); bathrobe (a raincoat will serve just fine); fancy clothes; expensive jewelry.

Our super-streamlined packing method, for the extra-light traveler who carries only a rucksack or an airline bag: Wear your bulkiest outfit — the suit, heavy sweater, boots, and/or overcoat. In addition to the clothes you wear, bring one more complete, coordinating set of clothes for a total of two complete outfits. For women these outfits should not include dresses, which are less versatile than separates.

If you're **packing light for a long trip,** remember that you can live for three months with the same amount of clothes as for a week. It's easy to rinse out shirts, socks, and undergarments in the sink.

The ideal raincoat is crushable, dark in color so that it never looks dirty, and looks great on you at any time. A handy combination would be such a raincoat, which can be rolled into a ball and stuffed into your suitcase or carry-on, and a down vest or parka that can be stuffed into its own little bag.

Bring a hat. A beret is our favorite for cold weather, since it always looks good on men or women. For warm places, bring a crushable hat with a visor.

The black rubber galoshes people used to wear over their shoes are perfect for traveling. They take up very little space in your luggage and will save you from the discomfort and health hazard of wet feet if you're caught in the rain (especially in a country like Ireland that is frequently rainy). Also useful are the transparent plastic boots that women can pull on over their shoes.

Light, loose-fitting clothing is best in **warm climates.**

Men should bring along a **sports coat** (except, perhaps, to South and Southeast Asia), and wear it en route. A tie can be rolled up and stuck in a corner of the suitcase.

Bring a good Swiss Army or other **folding knife** that includes a paring knife, bottle opener, and corkscrew. Pack it in your suitcase, not in your carry-on, purse or pocket, to avoid problems at airport security checkpoints.

Bring along a **net bag.** You'll find it useful for shopping, laundry, wet bathing suits, and presents you bring home for friends at the end of your trip.

If you are traveling extra light, you may have to **wear glasses** instead of contact lenses. The paraphernalia involved with contact lenses takes up more room, and the lenses are at constant risk of getting lost, damaged, or soiled.

If your contact lens case, soap dish, and toothbrush holder are of sturdy plastic you can send them **through the dishwasher** the day before you leave.

Laundry supplies could include concentrated liquid soap in a small plastic bottle, a string or stretchable clothesline, six little clothes-pins, an inflatable hanger or two, a sink stopper, a little clothes brush — or simply a bar of Ivory soap and a piece of string.

Many travelers bring along their own **towel and washcloth,** since hotel towels can be too few and too small. Yours should be a light weave, in order to dry quickly. A damp towel can dry hooked on to the handle of a suitcase or pack.

Prell shampoo can wash not only your hair, but your body and clothes as well. Because it's concentrated, one tube will last your entire trip.

We have carried a small pair of **binoculars** around the world and been glad to have them. They're useful in any number of ways, whether you're looking at distant elephants in Kenya, porpoises off the bow of your cruise ship, a bullfight in Spain or a concert in Central Park. Make sure to have four lens covers and a hard case.

Bring extra copies of your **passport photo** in case your passport gets lost or you wish to apply for a visa, an International Driver's License, a fishing license, or any special pass. You can always leave left-over copies with your new friends to remember you by.

A roll of **plastic garbage bags** (taken out of the box) has dozens of uses, including carrying trash, laundry, shoes, toilet articles, wet bathing suits, or spillables, or for grouping small things like socks and underwear that are otherwise easily lost in a suitcase. Such bags are especially useful when you're traveling with kids.

A small immersible **hot-water heater** can be a real boon. You'll enjoy being able to relax with a cup of tea or coffee in your hotel room. Be sure to bring a few tea bags or foil-wrapped packets of coffee, as well as the correct adaptor.

If you take any foreign-made items abroad you may have to pay duty on them when you return, unless you have **proof of prior possession.** An insurance policy, a receipt or bill of sale, or a jeweler's appraisal will be acceptable. You can register items with serial numbers, such as watches, cameras, and tape recorders, at the Customs office nearest you or at international departure areas. Keep the Certificate of Registration to use for your next trip.

PACKING

Well before your trip, **examine your luggage** to be certain it will hold up to the trip. It should be sturdy and rugged. Make sure zippers and handles are in excellent condition. Check seams for signs of strain. We think every item of luggage should have a shoulder strap — make sure the rings that hold it on are strong and secure.

If you have a large suitcase, and expect to be walking only at the airport, then a **set of wheels** on the suitcase makes sense. Otherwise, we have found them awkward, cumbersome, and inconvenient (they don't go up stairs, over curbs, or onto buses easily). We recommend that you take two small bags, with shoulder straps, rather than one larger one, if you think you'll have to carry them a lot.

Couples traveling together should bring **separate suitcases.** Each partner should include a few of the other's clothes in the suitcase, in case one of you loses your bag.

We feel that **20 pounds** is plenty to carry. Weigh your packed bag on a bathroom scale.

One way to pack light is to put out on your bed everything you absolutely have to take — and then **put half of it back** into your closet.

Make a **trial pack** a week before you leave. Examine everything for loose buttons, rips, and sagging hems. Put everything, including toilet articles and non-clothing items, in your suitcase, and walk around the house with it. If it's heavy now, it will seem three times as heavy a few days into your trip. Streamline before you go, to avoid having to jettison cargo during your journey!

Put liquids (shampoo, cosmetics, etc.) in **plastic screw-top containers,** which can be obtained in pharmacies, and tape the tops closed. Place them in plastic bags. We bring an extra roll of tape or some rubber bands along.

Inside each suitcase, tape your name, address, and itinerary, including addresses, phone numbers, and dates. Also enclose a list of the contents. This will ensure that you don't leave anything behind when you're repacking. (You can use this list again, refining it each trip.) Leave a copy at home in case your bag gets lost and you have to identify its contents.

Label the **outside of your suitcase** as well. If you are concerned about alerting potential burglars to the fact that your home is empty, you may wish to use your office address. Or you can tape an index card on your suitcase with your name on the outside and your address on the inside.

Put things you might **need in a hurry** on top of your suitcase or in your carry-on bag — bathing suit, warm sweater, flashlight, toilet kit, sleepwear.

Lock your luggage and keep the key in your pocket or handbag.

Take a space-saving tip from backpackers, and **roll your clothes** into neat cylinders to minimize wrinkles. This works well in suitcases, since you will end up with a lot of tight rolls that fit together well. If you roll several items of clothing together, you will end up with the least wrinkles.

Mark your suitcase in some distinctive way — with colorful tape, for instance — so that others cannot confuse your bag with theirs.

Whether you're traveling by plane, train, bus, or car, a **carry-on bag** makes sense, as a place to keep small, fragile, valuable, and frequently needed items.

Be sure to bring a **cover-up** if you'll be spending a lot of time at the beach or poolside.

Many travelers recommend fastening a **luggage strap** around each suitcase, both to make it distinctive from other similar bags and to discourage pilfering.

The following items should never be checked in a suitcase to travel in the baggage compartment:

traveler's checks	expensive jewelry
business documents	musical instruments
negotiable stocks &	eyeglasses
securities	matches or cigarette lighters
medicines	camera and film

Industy-wide regulations specify that each passenger may take on board a plane one suitcase or one garment bag. A woman may also carry a handbag. In fact, many passengers disregard these rules, the world over, and most airlines do not make a great effort to enforce them. Passengers come aboard with full-length mirrors, cellos, potted palms, microwave ovens, surfboards, and grandfather clocks!

This laxness has arisen because airlines have such an excellent record for safety and comfort. In an emergency, however, all of this extra baggage can become a safety hazard. During turbulence, heavy items can fall from the overhead compartments and injure people below. Lots of objects underfoot can impede an efficient evacuation or fuel a fire.

As of this writing, the Association of Flight Attendants has petitioned the Federal Aviation Administration to crack down on carry-ons, because of these safety issues. The F.A.A. is likely to issue a new order stiffening the regulations covering carry-ons.

We like to travel with just a carry-on bag, because we love the lightness and efficiency, and we love not having to wait the extra half hour for our luggage to emerge from the aircraft.

A carry-on bag must fit **under your seat** (20 by 16 by 9 inches), or if it is soft and filled with clothing only it may go in the overhead compartment.

Parents traveling with infants or toddlers are allowed to bring a **diaper-changing bag and a stroller.** If you feel you have enough to deal with already, with the child and the stroller, try to combine the baby's necessities and yours in one carry-on bag.

In your carry-on bag you should have the **essentials of life** for the first 2 hours of your trip, in case your suitcase does go astray. This would include toilet articles, medications, and a change of clothing.

In the dry air of an airplane cabin, many travelers complain of **dry skin.** Instead of moisturizer, you can use suntan lotion on your face and hands.

Wear your bulkiest clothing en route.

Other items the carry-on bag should contain:	
Camera and film	Lip balm and/or skin moisturizer
Reading matter	Slipper socks
Flashlight	Earplugs or eye shade, if desired
Documents	Nasal decongestant
Needs for first night	Travel alarm clock, set to
Contact lens supplies	destination time

Many women travelers claim that a full-skirted **traveling dress** is most comfortable and shows fewest wrinkles. Knits are also ideal.

A **jogging suit** is very comfortable to wear on a plane. Just be sure, though, to have a change of clothing in your carry-on bag. Someone we know wore a hot-pink sweatsuit for her flight to a conference in Europe, and her luggage went astray. She attended each of her seminars in the same pink outfit, because she had nothing else with her to wear. (Matters were made worse because sweatsuit material dries very slowly. After washing her outfit one night, she tried to hurry things up by hanging it over a lamp. She succeeded in burning a hole in her only outfit! See Chapter 15, "In an Emergency.")

CHAPTER SIX

WHAT TO DO BEFORE YOU GO

Prospective travelers tend to devote most of their time and energy to preparation for the actual trip and don't make provisions for the security of their homes. Don't forget to keep your house safe while you're gone.

Many of the following tips will require the help and assistance of a friend, neighbor, or relative. It would also be helpful to have someone serve as your emergency contact person while you're gone — to leave copies of your important information with this person, who will be ready to help if anything goes wrong.

If it seems like an imposition to ask someone to take in your mail and water your plants, offer your services in exchange as a house cleaner or errand person when you get back.

In the event that free help is not available, you may have to hire someone to live in, and look after, your home. In Chapter 23, "Useful Addresses," you will find an address for an organization that provides house-sitting services.

Whoever looks after your home and takes in your mail should be given a house key and a copy of your itinerary. Be sure you have this person's address and phone number.

How many people in your neighborhood need to know you are gone? We say the fewer the better. No one but the person who's looking after your home needs to know.

The most obvious signs of your absence are the most crucial. Have someone gather your mail faithfully every day and keep it safely in a bag or box in their home. Suspend deliveries of all kinds: newspapers,

UPS, the cleaner. No need to go into detail about your trip and your plans; you can telephone when you return and ask that service be resumed.

Another sign that indicates an empty and inviting house is a yard with grass four inches high or a driveway blanketed with a foot of snow.

Arrange to have someone mow your lawn once a week for the length of your trip. Get a recommendation from a friend for someone who does yard work. Pay this person in advance. Even if you'll only be gone seven days, you may not want to come home to a yard that immediately needs attention — extend your vacation a little by having your lawn cut on the day you're due back.

In the winter, engage a dependable person who will plow or shovel snow while you are gone. This person may ask for a refundable deposit, a small price to pay for a house that looks occupied and well maintained. If there isn't any need for snow removal, you should get your money back.

Pay all current bills if you will be gone for more than one billing period, or arrange to have someone make payment for you. This is especially important in the case of homeowner's and life insurance — be sure you're up to date on these well before you leave.

Even if you will be gone only for a short time, clear the refrigerator of all perishable foods, defrost the freezer (if necessary), and then turn it off or down. Also turn down the heat, water heater, and air-conditioning.

Empty the garbage, and run the disposal while you pack the car with your luggage, so that you won't return to a house full of bad odors.

Unplug small appliances, particularly the television, stereo, and any home computer equipment. Violent storms at any time of the year can bring down power lines and create a power surge that could start an electrical fire where such equipment is plugged in. An electrical fire could mean catastrophe if no one is in the house to alert the fire department immediately.

Make two lists of all the credit cards, traveler's checks, and ticket numbers you plan to carry with you, and the companies' emergency/theft phone numbers (see "Safety Numbers List," Chapter 22). Put one list in a sealed envelope and leave it with a trusted friend or relative or the person who is looking after your home. Take the other list in a sealed envelope and keep it apart from your documents. Can-

HOME SECURITY TIPS

Giving your house the appearance of occupancy is one of the best ways to prevent being the target of burglars. Go through the house carefully and use some or all of the tips below to keep the house safe during your absence:

■ Lock all doors and windows, especially those on the ground level and with access to a roof or patio.

■ If you have sliding glass doors you may want to make them extra secure with a locking bar (available at most hardware stores). In addition, be sure to close any curtains along the length of the glass doors.

■ Close curtains in the back of the house to prevent someone from boldly peering through the windows.

■ Put your lamps on automatic timers, if you have them; if not, leave some commonly used lights on in bedrooms and kitchens.

■ Always leave at least one bathroom light on and close the door. A bathroom is one place that could be occupied at any time of the day or night.

■ Close doors leading from one room to another. If someone is trying to look into the house to find out if anyone is at home, that person will only be able to see one room at a time.

■ Tune the radio to a 24-hour talk show station, and turn the volume up to a conversational level.

■ You can buy fake security system decals which can be applied to the doors leading into your house and say, "This house is protected by Acme Alarm Systems."

■ One of the very best things you can do is ask a trusted neighbor or friend to park their car in your driveway overnight, on the weekends, and for as much of the day as possible.

You will enjoy your trip more knowing that you have taken the time to make the house secure, and whether your neighbors know you are gone or not, *your* care will also keep *their* homes safe.

celling credit cards from a foreign or distant location could be nightmarish if you haven't taken this precaution.

Reconfirm domestic airline reservations 24 hours in advance, and international airline reservations 72 hours in advance.

On your way out the door call the hotel to confirm that there is a room waiting for you. Even if you have paid for everything in advance by cash or credit card, take the time to check your reservations. This is particularly important if you won't arrive at your hotel until after 6:00 p.m. A phone call will let the people at the hotel desk know when you plan to arrive, and assure that your room will be saved.

If the weather is bad on the day you plan to depart, call the airport to find out if flights have been cancelled or delayed. If flights are only being delayed, find out *exactly* when departure is planned.

CHAPTER SEVEN

GOING BY PLANE

(See also Plane Reservation Checklist, Chapter 22.)

By shopping around, you can fly for much less than others on the very same flight. The best fares belong to two types of travelers — those who are decided enough to make firm plans very early, and those who are flexible enough to get up and go at the last minute. If you start planning early, you will have the most options.

Airlines overbook their flights because they count on a certain number of people cancelling. If all of the people who reserved do decide to fly, someone will be "bumped" from the flight. You must reconfirm your flight three days before departure and arrive at the departure gate on time — or you may be the victim. (See below, "Getting Bumped.")

If you can make your reservation and purchase your ticket well in advance, the airline will give you a considerable discount — simply for the advantage of having your seats confirmed and paid for. This is why we recommend that you commit yourself early to your major transportation to and from your destination (but stay flexible once you're there!).

On the other hand, you may receive a deep discount if you are flexible enough to make plans at the last minute and take advantage of the "short-notice discounting" that frequently takes place with cruise ships, international flights, and, more and more often, domestic air routes. If a tour, cruise, or charter is not sold out close to departure time, the company may be desperate to fill those empty slots. These seats cannot be advertised, because that would be unfair to those passengers who paid full fare.

Discount travel operators have come into existence to make those seats available to you at 15 to 60 percent of full price. Most of these discount companies require a moderate annual membership fee that covers you and your family or a partner. For that cost you may have access to a hot-line listing bargain departures or a newsletter. Some companies include insurance. (For a list, see Chapter 23, "Useful Addresses," under Discount Travel Operators.)

This kind of arrangement is not for the person who wants to go to a certain place at a specific time; it is for the traveler who wants to head "someplace warm" on a cruise sometime during the winter, or on a charter flight to Europe sometime in July. Thus it is best for people who do not have rigid vacation schedules.

Certain people should not fly at all. Women whose pregnancy has progressed beyond 240 days or who are in danger of miscarriage should not travel by plane. People with serious health conditions (such as a recent heart attack or recent abdominal surgery) should consult their doctors regarding the safety of flying.

FINDING THE BEST FARE

Deregulation is the air traveler's best friend. It means you have a multitude of choices, even when the air fare wars aren't raging. The problem is that the average traveler isn't aware of the vast array of options, partly because the fares change too frequently to keep up with, and partly because the airlines would naturally prefer to sell at their higher fares. Sometimes even the reservations agent doesn't know every deal the airline is offering.

There may be **many different fares for the exact same seat** in coach class. Each fare is identified by a different code letter — Q, L, V, B, Y — and each has specific rules. For example, the Q fare may require a 30-day advance purchase, a stay that includes a Saturday night, and a 50 percent penalty if the trip is cancelled, and Tuesday and Wednesday are the cheapest days to travel. A V fare may be purchased two days ahead, and any day of the week but Friday and Sunday are cheapest, but the ticket is non-refundable and you must stay over a Saturday night.

The guiding principle of air fares is that **the lower the fare, the more restrictions** there will be, including expensive penalties if you cancel the flight within a certain date before departure.

Always ask the airline reservation clerk if the fare stated is the **cheapest available** — this person may not offer or seek that information otherwise. Ask whether flying midweek or Saturday is cheaper.

Midweek and midday travel may not only be cheaper than weekend travel, but it is also much less stressful. Or you may discover that if you can stay over a Saturday night, your fare will be greatly reduced. Ask your travel agent or the airline reservation clerk to investigate such possibilities.

Charter flights are much cheaper than regularly scheduled flights and for some people they make the difference between being able to afford a trip and not. You become a member of a group that rents an entire plane or just a block of seats on a regularly scheduled plane. The drawbacks to charter flights are that they are irregular — you have to be flexible regarding your departure date. And if you must cancel, you will not get your money back unless you have purchased cancellation insurance in advance.

Make sure the charter company you book with has an **escrow account.** Your money will stay in this account until your trip is completed. This will protect you if the charter company should "go under" between the time you pay for your ticket and complete your travel. Either ask the reservations agent, or have your travel agent check in *Jax Fax,* a reference book of charter companies.

You can also try to get a **last-minute seat** on a charter flight for even less than the already discounted fare. This requires maximum flexibility on your part, but if that suits you, it would be your best possible deal. Call a few charter companies to find out.

You may be able to fly free or at greatly reduced rates to cities all over the world if you become a runner for a **courier service.** Look in the Yellow Pages of a "gateway" city phonebook (San Francisco, New York, Seattle, Los Angeles, Philadelphia, etc.). The drawbacks to this are that you may not be able to take any luggage (just carry-ons) and that you have to be very flexible about when you go. But for people who like to travel light, this can be an extraordinarily good deal.

Inquire about **excursion rates** to Europe, which are often your best buy but come laden with restrictions. Excursion fares on international) or the even cheaper Super APEX fare. In the United States they may be known as Super Savers or Maxi Super Savers. You must buy the round-trip ticket from 21 to 30 days ahead of time. You must stay away a minimum of seven days and no more than 60 to 90 days. You'll be penalized for changes made before and during your trip.

Ask if there are **standby fares** on your route. These are less common now than a few years back, but you can still find them on international flights during "low season." The fares are greatly reduced but, unfortunately, it is very difficult to predict whether or not the plane will have seats available. Standby fares are only for those who can be completely flexible.

One well-kept secret, at this writing, is Eastern Airlines' **Sky Pass.** For a specified amount of money (currently $449) you can fly an unlimited number of miles within the continental United States for a 21-day period. For a bit more money (currently $599) you can include flights to Hawaii, Alaska, Canada, and the Caribbean, as long as all of your travels begin and end within that 21-day period. Delta, at this writing, has a similar deal. But you must ask about this; it is not advertised and reservation clerks have often never heard of it.

There are always certain airlines that give the best fares, but these can change from year to year. **Check the ads** in the travel section of your own newspaper and a major paper, such as The New York Times. Look for the smaller, newer companies. And remember that these airlines use the exact same equipment and adhere to the same safety regulations that the bigger names do.

Do not ignore the national airlines of **small foreign countries** — you may be pleasantly surprised. Singapore Airlines, for example, is one of the most luxurious yet reasonably priced airlines in the world.

Look in your newspaper for **promotional fares** the airline might offer for a short time only, perhaps to introduce a new route.

By using **secondary airports** (Newark instead of Kennedy, Oakland instead of San Francisco, Manchester instead of Heathrow or Gatwick), you can usually obtain a better fare.

Find out if a transatlantic flight will allow you to fly to **other European cities** without extra charge.

MAKING A RESERVATION

Use the phone, and remember that you have **many options** — you can telephone several airlines directly yourself and you can simultaneously have a travel agent working for you.

Telephone **at least three** different airlines (call 800-555-1212 to obtain their toll-free numbers) to find out differences in fares. If you call the airline in the early morning or late at night, you will have the best chance of getting through quickly and having a chance to work out the best deal with the agent.

Write **everything down** — the phone number, the name of the airline, the agent's name, the date and time you call, the flight numbers and times, and the price.

Make sure you know if your flight is **nonstop, direct** (it flies to your destination, but makes one or more stops along the way), or requires a change of planes (a **connection**). If you cannot fly nonstop or direct, try to arrange that your connecting flights be with the same airline. Although this will not ensure that the first gate will be near the connecting flight (arrival and departure gates can be located as much as a mile apart), the airline will feel some responsibility if your first flight is late.

Your travel agent or reservation clerk should allow for the time you will need **between flights** if you are changing planes. Do not take a flight that connects with less than 45 minutes for you to disembark and find the new gate. If you have only a half an hour to make the connection, and your first flight is late, you may miss the second plane.

Travel agents have **maps of all major terminals** in a book called the *North American Travel Planner,* which also indicates wheelchair accessibility of terminals. The *Official Airline Guide,* another tome on the travel agent's bookshelf, lists **minimum connecting times.**

SEAT SELECTION

Get your seat assignments and boarding passes as early as possible, especially if you have special requirements — you are disabled, you are traveling with small children, you are a business traveler who needs to get quickly off the plane.

With American Airlines, at this writing, you may get your seat assignment as soon as you make your reservation — as early as 330 days ahead of your departure date. With United Airlines, if you have a frequent flyer account, you may book your seats very early. With most airlines you can get your seat assignment 30 days in advance.

We like to sit right by the emergency exit. It makes us feel most secure, and the seats usually have a bit more leg-room.

The next most desirable (comfortable and accessible) seats are **aisle seats** toward the front, and **bulkhead seats.** The smoking section is in the rear of the aircraft. If you don't smoke, note that the back of the non-smoking section may be uncomfortably smoky.

Especially if you are traveling at holiday time, it will save you a great deal of time and aggravation if you have your seat assignment and boarding pass **before you reach the airport,** and check your baggage at curbside. (Don't use the curbside check-in, however, if you arrive at the airport late.)

A couple we know always books **an aisle seat and a window seat** in a three-seat row. Because a lone middle seat is always the last to be sold, these friends nearly always manage to fly with the luxury of an extra seat, with more leg-room, extra storage space, and an extra tray table. This is especially helpful if you are traveling with a baby.

If that middle seat is sold, its owner will undoubtedly let you sit together, since the middle seat has neither accessibility nor view. Make sure to give this person the choice of the window or aisle seat.

BUYING YOUR TICKET

Air fares are subject to **change without notice.** Once you buy your ticket, the airline cannot make you pay more if there is a fare increase. If the price of the ticket goes down in the same letter class in which you're booked, you will be eligible for a refund. If the fare goes down in a different letter class, however, then you may or may not receive some money back.

There are many reasons to purchase your ticket with a **credit card.** One is that you will have more luck getting reimbursed if the flight is cancelled. If you use an American Express card, you will have free flight and baggage insurance.

If you've purchased your ticket through a travel agent, call about two weeks before departure to find out **when you can pick up your ticket** and boarding pass. There may be restrictions regarding how early the agent can issue the latter.

When you pick up your ticket, **examine it carefully** to make sure that the information on it is correct. Check dates, times, flight numbers, connecting cities, and so on. Make sure there is a page for each leg of your journey. Become familiar with the ticket so that you know which part will be removed when.

As soon as you have your ticket, **write down the ticket number** and keep it in a safe place (see Chapter 22 for a "Safety Numbers Checklist"). Having a record of your ticket number will make reimbursement much easier if your ticket gets lost.

If you've reserved a discount flight, purchase **cancellation insurance** early. The airline will not reimburse you, except under extraordinary circumstances, if you cancel.

Find out if the airline will **mail you the ticket** directly, if you should buy the ticket at a travel agency, or if you must wait until you reach the airport to pick it up.

THE LAST FEW DAYS

Reconfirm your international flight **72 hours before departure** (a charter company can cancel your reservation if you don't), and to be extra sure, re-reconfirm one more time 12 hours before departure. Reconfirm a domestic flight **the day before departure.** Your travel agent may reconfirm for you, but make sure of this. If you have reconfirmed, and you show up at the gate on time, you are unlikely to get bumped. Write down the name of the agent you speak with, as well as the date and time of your call, in case there is any mixup.

If you have a cold, flu, or allergies, the American Medical Association warns that you may develop **painful ear and sinus problems** after experiencing cabin air pressure changes. Seriously consider postponing or cancelling your flight, and if that's impossible, use an oral decongestant an hour before landing or a nose spray or drops before and during descent.

If you are pregnant, check with your doctor before taking air sickness pills.

Try to get **plenty of sleep** the night before your trip.

Before leaving for the airport, call to find out if your flight is **on time.** Allow yourself plenty of extra time to get to the airport —twice the normal time if it is rush hour or Friday evening.

At the Airport

Follow the airline's instructions regarding **when to arrive** at the airport. Especially with a foreign flight, you will need the extra time — two hours for passing through the security check, which can be very slow during the holiday season, and for clearing customs. If you are there a little early, relax and enjoy the airport's shops and facilities and the opportunities for marvelous people-watching.

When you arrive at the airport, check updated information on **when the flight will leave.** If there is a line at the ticket counter, telephone the airline either on a courtesy phone or on the airline's toll-free number.

If there is going to be a long delay, and you cannot afford to wait, immediately begin **checking with a different airline** for another flight. It is our experience that you can nearly always get out.

If an international flight is seriously delayed, **do not pass through security and passport control too soon,** or you may be stuck in a departure lounge with many fellow passengers and few facilities.

If you are late, you do not have your ticket yet, and you need to check your baggage, go to the front of the line and **calmly explain your situation** to the person waiting there. (That person may be waiting for the same flight!) If he or she refuses to let you go ahead, you must appeal to the ticket agent or to the next person in line. If there is anyone else behind the counter, he or she may be able to ticket you. Be sure you have all necessary documents in your hand.

It is a sickening feeling to arrive at the ticket counter only to have the agent say, "Your flight's been called. You'd better run!" We have had many, many close calls, yet have always made our flight. The usual reasons people give for missing planes are that their connecting flight was late, they were caught in a huge holiday crush either on the road or at the airport — or they lingered too long in the duty-free shop! Most of these problems can be avoided with careful planning.

If your connecting plane is late, inform the ground personnel as soon as you arrive at the gate, and ask them to **telephone the connecting gate** or airline. Airlines do make an effort to hold a flight for confirmed passengers, if they know they are on their way.

Once you are in the airport, there are **TV monitors** listing flight arrivals and departures, and there will be numerous announcements ("TWA Flight 326 non-stop to Hong Kong is now ready for boarding; Flight 326 is now boarding; Last call for Flight 326; Flight 326 now departing....").

The number of airports with facilities for **parents traveling with children** is increasing. Ask at an information desk where you can change or nurse your baby. Some airports, as, for example, London's Heathrow, have actual nurseries with cribs, toys, and trained staff.

Every airport has **medical services** to handle emergencies, ranging from infirmaries to full-scale hospitals. Ask any member of the airport or airline staff.

LUGGAGE

Only a tiny percentage of the luggage taken aboard airplanes is lost or even misplaced, but because of the volume of bags involved, it is possible that this will happen to you. There are certain things you can do to increase the likelihood that your bags will end up where you do, and to minimize the hassle if they don't. (See also "If Your Luggage Gets Lost," below.)

When you pack, make a list of everything in each suitcase. If your suitcase goes astray, you may need to identify everything in it. And if it gets lost you will want a list of the contents in order to make a claim for compensation. Make a copy of each list and keep one inside each bag to serve as a checklist every time you repack.

Inside each item of luggage, **place a label** with your name and address. Add a copy of your itinerary, with dates and addresses, so that anyone finding your missing suitcase can easily track you down.

Lock every bag. If your suitcase is of a very common type, be sure to add some sort of **conspicuous identification** — stickers with your initials, contrasting tape, or a strap. Many experienced travelers strap their luggage so that it will not burst open if it's handled roughly.

Put a label on the **outside of your luggage** with your name on it. Add your office address, if you wish, instead of your home address, so that you won't alert possible burglars to your empty house.

Remove **old airline tags,** which can confuse luggage handlers and send your suitcase where you went on your last trip.

When you check your luggage, be sure you see the agent **tag each bag.** Make sure each item is checked through to your final destination, if possible (note that the airline abbreviation is correct), and that you have the matching baggage claim checks in your possession.

TIPS TO INCREASE LUGGAGE SAFETY

■ Make a list of every item packed in each bag. Keep one copy at home, and tape the other to the inside cover of the suitcase.

■ Write out your itinerary, with dates and addresses, and place a copy inside each bag.

■ Label each bag inside and out.

■ Do not carry valuables inside your checked luggage.

■ Do not carry liquids, cigarette lighters, or matches in your checked luggage.

■ Lock your luggage.

■ If your luggage is of a common type, give it some easily identifiable personalization — contrasting tape or a safety strap.

■ If your luggage is old or overstuffed, fasten a strap around it to keep it from opening.

■ Allow plenty of time for check-in.

■ Remove all old tags and stickers from your bag.

■ Check your suitcase through to your final destination, if possible.

■ Never leave your bags unattended.

■ As soon as you retrieve your bag from the baggage carousel, check the lock.

■ Do not leave your bags visible in a parked car.

Do not throw away your **claim check,** even if you have not used it on previous trips. In some airports you must have it in order to remove your suitcase from the baggage area.

Never leave your bags unattended — not just because they may be vulnerable to thieves, but also because airport security officials may remove them to examine them for explosives.

Do not subscribe to the "last on, first off" philosophy regarding luggage. Statistics show that the luggage that is lost was usually checked in at the last minute.

SECURITY

Although security clearance seems like an annoying inconvenience, it is vitally important in keeping your flight safe. If passengers cooperate the procedure should be smooth and efficient.

The security officers will examine your carry-ons and handbags with X-ray equipment. You will pass through a metal detector. Sometimes a jackknife in your pocket will set off the alarm, and for this reason you may want to pack it in your luggage.

Some countries are more vigilant than others. At some airports, passengers will be **personally searched** for weapons by male or female security guards. They will even search your baby's stroller. Sometimes your luggage is searched before it is placed on the aircraft.

If you do not have a film shield, **remove your camera and film from your carry-on bag** (which will be scanned by the X-ray) and carry it through the check-point or hand it to the security guard. For this reason it is convenient to keep your film in a zip-closure plastic bag or to have both camera and film in a padded bag that can be easily removed from your carry-on.

Do not make **jokes about terrorism.** Security personnel will not find them funny.

The Department of Transportation requires that the airlines provide a **no-smoking seat** for every passenger that has met the check-in deadline. If there are not enough seats to accommodate all the non-smokers who have checked in on time, the airline must expand the no-smoking section.

There is **no smoking** allowed on any commercial aircraft designed to seat fewer than 30 passengers. There is no smoking allowed in any aircraft when it is on the ground. And cigar and pipe smoking are forbidden on all commercial flights.

Airlines request that you do not use or refill the **transparent type of lighter** containing regular lighting fluid during your flight, as this type can spill and flare.

Before sitting down, **take a blanket and pillow** from the overhead rack. These tend to disappear once the flight is underway.

Before take-off, fasten your seat belt snugly **around your hips** (not your stomach), and make sure you know how to remove it quickly.

If you are traveling with an infant or a toddler, hold him on your lap, **outside of your seat belt,** during take-off and landing.

Despite airlines' relatively good safety record, it is smart to **be prepared for emergencies.** Read the safety instructions in your seat pocket, which will inform you as to emergency procedures, emergency exits (notice where they are, and count how many seats are between your seat and the nearest exit), and how to operate safety equipment. Listen to the flight attendant's brief explanation of safety procedures, even if you've heard it a hundred times before. Pay particular attention, if you are flying over water, to how to put on and inflate the life vest — this tends to be the point to which passengers in an emergency wish they had paid attention.

If you are traveling with a child, note that the procedure calls for you to **put on your oxygen mask first,** and then help the child put hers on.

TIPS TO INCREASE COMFORT EN ROUTE

- Sit in an aisle seat toward the front of the aircraft.

- Do not wear tight clothing or shoes.

- Slip out of shoes and elevate feet (on carry-on or briefcase stowed beneath seat in front of you).

- Eat lightly.

- Put a pillow behind the small of your back.

- Drink plenty of non-alcoholic, non-caffeine beverages. A glass of water every hour is good.

- Take an occasional stroll around the cabin.

- Bring a sweater or jacket — airplane cabins are usually cool.

- Use lip balm on lips, moisturizer for skin, and eye drops or contact lens lubricant to combat the effects of cabin dryness.

- Bring a toilet kit so that you can freshen up in the rest room before arriving at your destination.

- Bring along a cassette player with earphones (but not a radio, which will interfere with aircraft navigation systems).

The **air pressure** in your aircraft is equivalent to that at 8,000 feet above sea level. This is higher than where most people live, and can cause discomfort. If your ears bother you during takeoff and landing (caused when the middle ear is affected by changes in air cabin pressure), try yawning, chewing gum, or this: pinch your nostrils shut, inhale, close your mouth, and try to gently blow your nose.

On a long flight, **put your feet up** on your carry-on or briefcase stowed under the seat in front of you. Slip out of your shoes (your feet will swell during the flight) and put on some slipper socks. Place a pillow behind the small of your back.

In addition to hoisting their feet up, people with varicose veins should **stroll down the aisle** of the aircraft periodically.

EXERCISES EN ROUTE

The following exercises, which can be done in your seat with your seat belt loosely fastened, are recommended by American Airlines. They stimulate circulation and stretch and relax cramped muscles. Try them with kids. They are especially valuable on a transoceanic flight.

Lean your head as far forward as possible, feeling the stretch down the back of your neck. Lean head to the side, keeping face front, and feel the stretch down the side of the neck. Lean to the other side.

Let head drop back, with jaw relaxed, and gaze at the overhead compartment of the row behind yours. Arch your upper back.

Hug yourself, placing your right hand on your left shoulder and your left hand on your right shoulder. Lean your head forward and pull your shoulders forward.

Roll your shoulders forward simultaneously, and then roll them back, arching your back. Then roll them in circles, one by one, toward the front and then toward the back.

Grab the back of your left armrest with your right hand and twist your upper body around to look behind you. Do the same with the other side.

Press your elbows down onto your armrests as hard as you can.

Reach up toward your light with one arm and then the other.

Loosen your seat belt, and then lean over to the floor, stretching your arms as far as possible. Sit up slowly.

Tighten the muscles in your buttocks and then release.

Lift one foot off the floor by lifting your thigh about an inch from the seat. Rotate your foot in one direction and then in the other. Repeat with the other foot.

The air in the cabin will be **very dry.** Accept all of the flight attendants' offers of free beverages — choose plain non-carbonated water or fruit juices, instead of caffeinated or alcoholic drinks (which will tend to dehydrate you). Bring a small tube of moisturizer or suntan lotion in your carry-on bag, along with some lip balm and some eye drops or contact lens lubricant. If your eyes begin to smart, take out contact lenses and wear glasses.

If you're not crazy about airline food, take a tip from a well-traveled friend of ours. When she ordered **the vegetarian meal,** she found it to be much more attractive and delicious — perhaps because it was specially made — than the regular meals her seatmates were served. You must order it when making your flight reservation.

Other alternative menus include kosher, diabetic, low-salt, low-calorie, low-fat, high-protein, bland, Moslem and Hindu meals. With all of these, you must order in advance. The airline does not carry special meals otherwise.

Airline regulations stipulate that the only **liquor consumed aboard the aircraft** must be served by your flight attendants. Service will be ended to any passenger who appears intoxicated.

International flights often offer a chance to purchase **duty-free gifts.** Liquor is generally more expensive, however, than in the United States. Know your prices ahead of time so that you know if you're getting a good deal!

If you are traveling alone it is important to **stay alert.** A friend of ours paid no attention to an announcement that her plane was arriving in Cleveland. Bound for Pittsburgh, she had not realized that her flight included a stop. Believing she was at her destination, she got off the plane. Only after 15 minutes in the airport did she realize she was in the wrong city. Luckily, she was able to re-board her plane and continue on to Pittsburgh. Most airports look the same, after all, so it is important to know the exact details of your flight.

Do not leave your purse, billfold, passport, or other valuables on your seat when you get up to stroll around. You should **have your passport on your person** at all times.

Airplanes are terrible places to try to sleep. If you are flying at night, you may wish to **bring along ear plugs** and/or an eye mask. Try to find an empty block of three seats where you can stretch out. You will need every minute of sleep you can get if you are flying all night and arriving in the morning.

Purchase an **inflatable neck pillow.** This hooks around your neck and gives your head restful support.

A sleep-inducing trick that never fails us: Close your eyes and rest your head comfortably against the wall or the edge of the seat. Relax your body. Now imagine that a great, soft broom is slowly sweeping your thoughts out of your head. As each new thought appears, the broom sweeps it away. The broom slowly empties all of the thoughts out of your head, and finally it sweeps away your consciousness itself. You will most likely be asleep; if not, try again.

FEAR OF FLYING

An estimated 25 million people, including someone as tough as boxer Muhammad Ali, share a fear of flying. For some it's the height that brings on the dizziness and panic; for others it's the loss of control; for still others it's a fear of engine failure or the sensation of being confined. We've been plagued with this fear ourselves, and yet have managed to fly anyway. Some tips to help you control the problem:

■ Arrive at the airport in plenty of time, to minimize stress.

■ Sit toward the front of the aircraft, where the ride will be smoother and quieter.

Another way to cope with the **fear of flying** is to understand exactly what an airplane is doing when it makes strange noises.

During take-off and landing, you will notice elaborate adjustments being made to the shape of the wings by movement of the flaps. These are used to increase uplift during take-off and to aid landing later. The flaps move in degrees during landing. The passenger hears the movement and the rushing sound caused by increased resistance.

Every aircraft can start and take off safely even if one engine fails, and the pilots are prepared to deal with this.

Just after take-off you will hear the wheels being retracted, sounding like the crashing of heavy doors.

The aircraft will probably bank just after take-off, as it goes into a curve. Inside the cabin things will feel level, but you will see the earth outside one side of the aircraft and the sky out the other.

Although "air pockets" do not exist, some strong vertical air movements may jostle the plane. The passenger will feel the jolt. The aircraft is designed to have the elasticity it needs and has been put through the severest of tests.

More than 100 miles before reaching the destination a pilot on a long-distance flight will begin the descent. The air traffic controller is deciding where in the sequence of inbound and outbound flights this particular aircraft will come. Jets are separated by three miles horizontally and 1,000 feet vertically.

If the airport is very busy, the air traffic controller will put the incoming jet into a holding pattern, an area up to 20 miles from the airport where jets can circle around a radio beacon at different levels. The air traffic controller will guide each craft, 1,000 feet at a time, down the various "floors" of the hold (there may be five floors at a busy airport).

About five miles before the airport the landing flaps assume their landing configuration and the wheels are lowered. The passenger will hear a rumbling sound as the wheels lock into place.

Sometimes a pilot makes a rough landing on purpose, if the runway is rainy. The loud noise is of the engine's thrust being reversed to help brake the plane. You may cheer — you made it!

■ Sit in an aisle seat, so that your attention will be directed toward the activity in the center of the aircraft, not to the great space out the window.

■ Bring along a good book — a thrilling page-turner, if possible.

■ Relax as fully as you can. Imagine you are in a serene place.

■ If you are still afraid, tell the flight attendant. It may help simply to feel less alone.

Most of those who share this phobia are fearful only during **take-off, turbulence, and landing,** since it is difficult to be nervous during the tedium of a smooth flight. Remind yourself during take-off that the difficult period will soon be over.

A program called *Help for the Fearful Flyer,* designed by Captain T.W. Cummings, is available in both an audio-video cassette and a book, published in 1987 by Simon and Schuster.

Knowledge may be the best antidote to the fear of flying. If you are flying over land (across the United States or Europe, for example), you might bring along a portable atlas, so that you can look out the window and roughly follow the airplane's route. If it's clear you may become absorbed in the landscape despite your fear. If it's not clear, look at the clouds and determine what type they are.

JET LAG

Jet lag is a state of extreme fatigue and disorientation caused by crossing several or many time zones with such speed that the body cannot adjust to the new schedule. (One does not suffer jet lag after flying north/south, only after flying east or west.) It is as if the body were catching up in the time it would have taken it to get there over land.

The condition is characterized by headaches, constipation, insomnia, nervousness, irritability, sluggishness, and forgetfulness, most of which seem to be symptoms typical of sleep deprivation. One famous U.S. diplomat blamed what he considered the major misjudgment of his career on fatigue caused by jet lag.

Some people seem to be immune to jet lag; others can be laid low by it for more than a week. Babies and children can adapt relatively fast while older travelers report that they suffer more from jet lag as years go by.

ANTI-JET LAG DIET

A few days before your departure date, begin to alter your body rhythms in preparation for the new time zone. You can reset the body's clocks by carefully rearranging eating and sleeping patterns. It is not as hard as it sounds. If you are flying east on a transatlantic or transcontinental flight, three days before your departure have a "feast day," eating heartily of a high-protein breakfast and lunch and a high-carbohydrate supper. At the same time, stop drinking tea or coffee. Two days before you leave, have a "fast day," eating the same type of meal but keeping portions small. One day before your trip, have another "feast day." On departure date, get up early, eat lightly during the day, drink a lot of water, and have several cups of strong coffee or tea at six p.m. Get a good night's sleep.

If you're headed west, it's the opposite — start three days early with a "fast" day, alternate feast and fast days, and then eat well on your departure date. People we know say this diet does work, especially to relieve the digestive problems that typically accompany the beginning of a trip.

Jet lag after flying east seems to be more long-lasting and more difficult to cope with than jet lag after flying west, perhaps because it is harder for the body to adapt to missing a few hours than to adding them on.

The expert on jet lag is Dr. Charles F. Ehret, who at the Argonne National Laboratory in Argonne, Illinois, has been researching the problem of jet lag and its solutions for the U.S. government. His book, *Overcoming Jet Lag* (New York: Berkley Books, 1984), not only has many good tips regarding jet lag and in-flight comfort, but it also sets out a careful regime, starting a few days before your flight, that will help minimize the effects of jet lag (see box).

Here are a few other tips to help you cope.

■ Never schedule an important meeting within 24 hours of your arrival if you are flying across three or more time zones. Try to plan your trip so that you have a day to begin adjusting, or you will be at a disadvantage during your meeting.

■ Try to plan to arrive at your destination at bedtime.

■ Get plenty of sleep the night before departure and the first night of your trip.

■ Sleep, if at all possible, during your journey.

■ Dehydration can intensify the problems of jet lag. Try to drink at least one non-caffeinated, non-alcoholic beverage every hour while on the plane.

GETTING BUMPED

Getting bumped is not as common as you may fear. According to statistics from the Department of Transportation, in 1984 only 4.55 passengers were bumped for every 10,000 that flew. Holidays are the time when you are most likely to be bumped.

Overbooking is legal because so many passengers don't show up for the reservations they've made that if the airlines were required to hold their seats they'd lose a tremendous amount of money. With the aid of computers, the airline figures out how many no-shows have occurred on each flight, and based on this number it estimates how many seats they can overbook.

If the airplane is full, the carrier is required to seek volunteers who will give up their seats in exchange for compensation. If an insufficient number of passengers volunteers, the airline will "bump" those still waiting at the gate.

If the airline can get you on a flight that arrives within an hour of your original flight, then it need not pay you any compensation. If you arrive one to two hours later than originally scheduled, the carrier must pay you, in addition, the cost of your ticket, up to $200 ($400 for international flights). If you arrive more than two hours late, the carrier will pay double the cost of your ticket, up to $400 ($800 for international flights).

Sometimes you will not be offered cash, but you will be given a free ticket. If you prefer cash, you can insist upon it.

In order to receive compensation, you must hold a confirmed and reconfirmed reservation, and you must have checked in by the airline's deadline (ask what this is — it can vary from 10 to 30 minutes before departure for domestic flights, and more for international flights).

You are not entitled to compensation if you did not follow the rules regarding reconfirming and checking in or if you are bumped from a commuter plane (less than 60 seats) or from a plane flying to the U.S. from a foreign country. Usually, in the latter case, you will be compensated to half the cost of your airline ticket, but that is in the company's discretion — some foreign carriers will not reimburse you at all.

Some airlines promise that they will not bump a **full-fare passenger.** Check with your travel agent.

Even if you have reconfirmed and arrived at the airport on time, you must arrive **at the gate** by the time the airline has set or you may be bumped.

VOLUNTEERING

If you have a flexible schedule, you may not mind giving up your seat, arriving a few hours later than scheduled, and receiving compensation besides. DOT rules now require that airlines solicit volunteers before they can bump a passenger.

Before accepting compensation, find out when the next flight is on which you can have a confirmed seat.

If the airline offers cash as compensation, make sure it will be enough to cover your expenses — hotel and meals, for example, if you have to wait for a morning flight. If it is offering free tickets instead of cash, find out what restrictions these tickets carry. You may be able to negotiate your compensation.

The airline is required to give you the check or tickets immediately. Once you have accepted them, you will have a hard time demanding more later, so you must make a quick and accurate analysis of your needs.

CANCELLATIONS

Most airlines no longer routinely provide hotel rooms, meals and free phone calls to passengers facing long delays or cancellations. Now these services will be offered only if the flight is diverted to an unscheduled location.

If your flight is seriously delayed, you may be able to insist that the airline clerk get you a seat on another airline. Before committing yourself to this second flight, however, make sure that it really will fly, and that your original carrier will pick up any fare increase.

If there is a long line at the ticket counter you may find it easier to check with other airlines yourself.

If your flight is cancelled, the airline will usually arrange passage for you on the next flight out to your destination. Some discount airlines, however, may make you wait for their own next flight.

IF YOUR LUGGAGE IS LOST

If your suitcase does not turn up, file a formal claim with the airline immediately, before leaving the airport — even though you have a week to do so. You will have to list the lost items, including their date of purchase and cost. Keep your claim form, baggage check, and ticket until you get reimbursed — it may take six months.

For lost, damaged or delayed baggage, the liability limit is **$1,250 per passenger,** on all domestic flights on large aircraft (or on smaller aircraft included on the same ticket with large aircraft).

If the company estimates that your loss was **less than this,** it may pay you much less, or even nothing.

You can purchase **excess valuation coverage** to increase the airline's liability. This tends, in our opinion, to be too expensive (as much as $2.00 for every $100 of extra coverage). Baggage insurance available at airport insurance counters may be a better deal, covering your bags not just while they are at the airport but throughout your entire trip. Your own homeowner's insurance may also be adequate.

The airline will not accept liability for damage to **fragile items,** unless, possibly, they are packed in the original factory-sealed carton, or are in special padded cases. Be sure you carry items such as musical instruments on board with you, or insure them separately.

If your bag is delayed, the airline may reimburse you for moderate **out-of-pocket expenses** for items such as toilet articles and essential items of clothing. This payment will be small, at least initially, because the airline anticipates (and is usually successful at) reuniting you and your bag in a day or two.

If you are **far from home** and your bags are lost the airline may pay you more money than if you are returning home.

If you check in at least 15 minutes before departure time, and your bag doesn't get on your flight, the airline usually assumes responsibility for **delivering it to you** when it finally arrives. If you check in later than 15 minutes, they may not. Some will not even check baggage that late.

If your bag doesn't show up **within 3 days,** its chances of being recovered diminish markedly. Most airlines will search for it for about 30 days.

On international flights, the Warsaw Convention limits the amount of liability to just **$9.07 per pound** of luggage. You may wish to insure your bags for more.

IF YOUR TICKET IS LOST

Fill out a lost-ticket application. It is much easier if you jotted down the ticket number; otherwise you'll have to trace the number through your travel agent. Since the ticket is good for one year, you won't be reimbursed within that time.

HIJACKING

Non-stop wide-bodied aircraft are statistically less likely to be hijacked than narrow-bodied single-aisle aircraft. As of this writing, no multi-aisle plane has ever been hijacked, perhaps because hijackers would have difficulty maintaining control of the passengers on such planes.

Passengers in first-class sections are generally treated more harshly in a hijacking situation than those farther back.

Certain airlines, such as Swissair, SAS, and Qantas, have not been targeted by hijackers, perhaps because their countries maintain neutral postures in world politics.

Passengers in aisle seats are more likely to be singled out by hijackers than those in other seats.

CHAPTER EIGHT

GOING BY BOAT

Once only the most hearty (or foolish) of souls would *choose* to travel over the ocean or transcontinental rivers as a passenger on a vessel of any kind. A lot has changed about passengers and passenger ships in the centuries since native Americans carved canoes out of tree trunks and the Pilgrims embarked on a voyage for freedom.

Now we have ocean liners that resemble small cities, enormous ships that steam past the once-fearsome Straits of Magellan or up the glacier-bordered Inland Passage without a break in the luxury service or lavish entertainment. Visions of acres of deck chairs, top-quality performers, fresh sea air, and the chance to view porpoises or flying fish combine to draw the traveler who can afford it to an ocean voyage purely for fun.

Today anyone with the inclination and the money can travel by boat in three different ways: on a trans-Atlantic or transoceanic crossing, on a cruise ship, and as a passenger on a freighter. Each offers a different type of atmosphere and level of activity, and you will find a different type of fellow passenger on each.

A transoceanic voyage generally attracts an older, more moneyed, sophisticated, worldly person, and the shipboard activities will reflect the intellectual, cultural, and social demands of these customers. Cruise passengers aren't necessarily less affluent or sophisticated, but they seek a more casual, totally relaxing experience (fun, entertainment, and a variety of people and activities). Those who travel by freighter are not looking to catch some rays or learn volleyball; they pay by the day to accompany a cargo vessel and her crew on a voyage that could begin in Chicago and end in Amsterdam, or could originate in New York and wind up in Hong Kong. A freighter does not offer the amenities and amusements one might find on any passenger vessel.

Most of this chapter is about travel on an ocean-going passenger vessel, with an introductory emphasis on the cruise as a vacation option, and a short section on freighter travel. To our way of thinking, going by boat is one of the most enjoyable travel choices a vacation shopper can take.

CRUISES

Long considered the bastion of the rich and famous, cruise vacations are now more popular than ever because of attractive pricing, special deals, and a myriad of possible destinations and shipboard activities. Where else can a smart vacation shopper get transportation, accommodations, all meals and every conceivable kind of entertainment, all for one prepaid price? Your choices and the cost can vary from an around-the-world-in-90-days junket to an 8-hour excursion up the Mississippi River.

Thanks in large part to the incredible popularity of the television series "Love Boat," people everywhere are considering a cruise as an attractive, luxurious, and affordable vacation. Every ship offers its passengers many choices in activities, ports of call (or none), meals and entertainment, sports and recreational facilities, and social gatherings. There is something for everyone: the young married couple, singles, children, and the retired. No matter how much you pay for your cabin you are entitled to the same amenities as every other passenger. And because you pay for it in advance, there are very few surprises or hidden expenses.

If you think a cruise vacation might be of interest to you, go to your favorite travel agent with some idea of what you like and dislike in a vacation. A travel agent will be invaluable to you in deciding on, and booking, a cruise vacation. Before you go, look over the travel section of your Sunday paper and various travel magazines so that you can familiarize yourself with special promotions, cruise themes, and ports of call. The travel agent will show you full-color brochures and cruise options. Solicit your travel agent's opinions on various ships and cruise lines — if he or she can't answer your specific questions then you should be directed to someone who can. You need to know all the latest deals, price breaks, special excursions, renovation plans, and which ship or ships will be best for you and your situation.

What you need to keep in mind as you plan a cruise vacation is: *how long would you want to cruise for, how much can you reasonably afford to spend per person, are there specific ports you do (or don't) want to see,* and *are you flexible as to where you go and the ship you go on?* There are as many choices as there are destinations and ships taking passengers, but if you consider the following points it may be easier to narrow down your choices.

■ Longer cruises (more than 7 to 10 days) are generally more formal in style and atmosphere. The shorter cruises (overnight to a week or 10 days) are generally more casual, and are often known as "fun" ships. In the same way, longer cruises are more likely to attract an older, more mature, more distinguished clientele, and shorter cruises are a haven for younger people and families.

■ When you first see the cost for a cruise vacation it may seem like a staggering amount of money. But remember that the price represents your total vacation expense, including transportation and accommodations, activities and entertainment. Your out-of-pocket expenses will include tips to ship personnel at the end of the voyage (more on that later), any items you buy on board or on-shore, and any shore excursions you may want to take. If you do some quick division, you will find that a cruise vacation is comparable in price to most pay-as-you-go land vacations.

■ You make your own decisions on a cruise vacation. You can take advantage of the many activities or sit in a lounge chair for a week and soak up the sun. You are free to explore any ports your ship calls at, but it is up to you. Some cruise vacations don't make any port stops at all; some may stop at a number of ports, long enough for you to enjoy some sightseeing; and some may spend an equal amount of time on the ocean and in port. Check the cruise itinerary to get the specifics about length and kind of port stops, and whether they cost extra.

■ If you can be flexible as to where you go and what ship you go on, you can save yourself some money. Some cruise lines offer great deals to people who will fill the empty cabins on various ships and cruises. It works something like this: you decide the price range, and the ship, and the cruise line will decide which cruise to put you on; or you can decide the price range and the cruise, and the cruise line will assign you to a ship. The savings could be considerable because the cruise lines want the ship to be as full as possible before they set sail.

■ Advance planning is as important to a successful cruise as any other vacation. If you are able to decide on, and book, a cruise well enough in advance (and you don't much mind where your cabin is) you can save some money. The first cabins to be booked on many cruises are either the most expensive or the least expensive. When you consider that every passenger is entitled to the same service and offerings, it makes sense that you could realize some significant savings by choosing a less expensive cabin.

■ Some cruise lines offer discounts to those who book "early," which can increase your savings even more if you have already put your dibs on a less expensive cabin. Your travel agent will know of any such deals, and they may even be advertised in the newspapers and magazines.

■ There is a chance that the travel agent will try to sell you a package for more than you have budgeted. Listen to the pitch, but be firm about your own requirements. Make it clear that you want the most vacation for the least amount of money. Ask about any "fly free" (or practically free) deals that the cruise lines offer to make it easy for you to reach the port of departure. It is common practice now for cruise lines to offer round-trip airfare to passengers for free or at a *greatly* reduced rate.

■ Ask what the fare would be for children accompanying an adult or adults or for a large cabin with four people. Ask about any special promotions offered by cruise lines for the area or type of cruise you are interested in. The travel agent is there to help you, and if you show an intelligent interest in your anticipated cruise, he or she can be a great resource.

After you have chosen your cruise or crossing date, you will choose a cabin or cabins (see below), and be asked to leave a deposit that represents a percentage of the total fare. This confirms your spot and reserves your cabin (or at least a cabin in the price range you have chosen). You will have to pay the remainder of the ticket price at some point before departure, and some lines ask you to pay in full when you book your ticket.

If you haven't yet been assigned a cabin, you will be given a cabin number when your entire fare has been paid.

Look carefully at your ticket when you receive it just to be safe: check to be sure that the ship, cabin assignment, date of departure, and point of departure are what you expect. Your ticket will outline the cruise line's policy on everything from luggage restrictions to what will happen if the cruise is unexpectedly cut short. The ticket is really a contract — read all the fine print so that you understand what to expect from the cruise lines and what they expect from you as a passenger.

The ticket will also outline the policy on **passenger cancellations.** If you have to cancel (whatever your reasons may be) and you can let the cruise line know well enough in advance, you probably will not be penalized with cancellation charges — you should receive back the entire price of your ticket. But the closer you get to the departure date, the greater the chance that the cruise line will keep a portion of your fare, as a deterrent against capricious reservations. Cruise ships are not like planes — they cannot be overbooked because they only have so much room and they ask for payment in order to reserve a place for every passenger.

Certainly emergencies arise, and you might well have to charge your plans. If you cannot go at the last minute for health reasons, and your doctor will verify that, the cruise line may give you a full refund. But when you book a cruise or crossing it is assumed that you know and understand the provisions under which the ticket as sold. Many travel agents sell *trip insurance* for a small fee, which will protect you against losing money if you can't make the trip. Trip insurance is an especially good idea if you are traveling by boat, not only because you generally must pay in advance, but because there are almost always expensive cancellation penalties. The ticket, and your travel agent, will give you all the specifics, but the burden is on you to know and understand the cancellation policy for the trip you book.

RED TAPE

No passport is necessary for cruises to the Bahamas, the Caribbean, Mexico, and Canada. If you will be sailing to Mexico, you may need a Mexican Tourist Card. You should obtain one, if necessary, from your travel agent or the nearest Mexican consulate before you leave. If you will be visiting any countries other than these, then you are obligated to obtain a passport and any necessary visas just like a land traveler.

YOUR CABIN

Choosing a cabin can be less mysterious with the help of a travel agent. Realize ahead of time that your accommodations will be small — a lot smaller than they appear in the brochure, and less than half the size of a conventional hotel room. If the cruise line is true to its advertising you won't be spending much time there except to sleep and change clothes, but be prepared for cabin intimacy.

The cabins on most older ships are slightly larger than on most new ships, and a bit more gracious and elegant. Newer ships offer cabins that are practically identical in size and shape, unless you have booked a suite or a deluxe accommodation. You pay more for a cabin that is closer to the public rooms and main decks. If you don't mind walking up a flight or two of stairs or taking an elevator, you can get the same cabin for less.

Each cabin will have a bathroom, some drawer space, a dressing table, a closet, and beds. It is now standard for each cabin to have bathroom facilities. The bathroom will be even smaller (proportionately) than your cabin — and only one person can really be in there at a time. There probably won't be a bathtub, just a shower stall. The beds, as you will see in the ship's brochure, are most likely twin beds. The floor plans on some ships will allow you to push the two beds together, but that will drastically reduce the amount of space in the room. Also offered (in tourist class or in cabins for four passengers) are bunk beds and Pullman beds that flip up during the day to give you more room. If you want a double or queen-sized bed, you'll need a larger room, which will undoubtedly cost you more money.

Before you choose your cabin find out where the public rooms are in relation to cabins. If you like to get to bed early, you won't want to be near the disco or bar, and if you like to sleep late you shouldn't be near the dining room or upmost decks. Rooms near stairs or the elevators may be noisy when people go to and from their cabins, as are rooms near the ship's engines and the kitchen.

If you think you may get seasick, book a cabin away from the bow, on the lower decks, and toward the center of the ship (not looking out at the sea). A good analogy is a tall tree swaying in the wind: the tree sways less lower down on the trunk and in the middle than higher up. Of course, all modern cruise ships are equipped with stabilizers to lessen the effects of rough waters.

Inside rooms may be a bit darker and perhaps a little smaller than an outside room, and they are generally less expensive. Outside rooms have a window or porthole (sealed shut because of the air conditioning) and will cost more. Some outside rooms have portholes that face a deck or promenade, and passengers will be walking and talking past your window for the entire trip. There are of course curtains, but if you appreciate privacy and you would like an outside room, you should be sure that your window will give you a view only of the ocean, and not of other passengers.

WHAT TO TAKE

You pack for a cruise or crossing in much the same way as you would for any other vacation. It is assumed that you have done a little research as to where you are going and what kind of climate to expect, both in port and on the water. A good, comfortable pair of shoes is as important on a cruise vacation as on a land vacation — you'll do more than your share of walking even if you never leave the ship. The night air on the water can be cold, and so can the interior of the ship, so be sure to bring at least one wrap or sweater to fight off the chills.

Try to coordinate your wardrobe to minimize the need for cleaning and laundry services. If your trip is a short one, your clothes may not need cleaning. If you are thinking of laundering items yourself, remember that there will be hardly enough space in your cabin for a travel clothesline. Certainly you'll want to bring sportswear and two or three dressy outfits: for women this could mean any formal dress or gown, and for men it usually means just a dark business suit. Very few cruises are so formal that men should pack a tuxedo and women their ball gowns, but your travel agent will know the level of formality on your particular cruise.

Every ship's brochure will make clear what the **electrical compatibility** will be, if any, with your various traveling appliances (hair dryers, razors, curling irons). Travel irons are prohibited on many ships not only because they require more electricity, but because they pose a tremendous fire risk. Depending on where your ship was built and the countries it primarily serves, you may or may not need a voltage converter. If this is not covered in promotional materials, be sure to get an answer from your travel agent or someone at the cruise lines.

Any **luggage** you take on a cruise will be subject to the same abuse as it is on planes, cabs, and trains, perhaps even more so. Pack your things in durable luggage. The hard items such as shoes should line the outside (near the zipper) of your bag. Protect breakables in zip-closure bags.

MEALS AND ACTIVITIES

On a cruise or crossing you will be offered more in the way of food and activity than any mortal being could eat or absorb. You will surely be astounded by the number and variety of each.

The larger ships offer two sittings for every meal, with approximately two hours separating each sitting. The second sitting usually attracts a more gregarious, fun-loving group. You can often request a sitting when you book or pay for your tickets, and you may even be able to get your table assignment.

If you haven't been **assigned to a table** by the time you arrive on ship, approach the dining room steward as soon as you get a chance. You can choose a table for two, four, eight, and in some cases, ten or twelve. You can ask to be seated with friends and traveling companions, you can ask to sit at a large table, or you can ask for a table for two. One frequent cruiser we know recommends choosing a table for eight — there's sure to be someone you hit it off with. Whatever size table you choose, you must arrive promptly for each meal. No one at your table will be served until everyone has arrived.

If you find yourself at a table that you are unhappy with, ask the maitre d'hotel for a change. Such a request can usually be honored when it is made persuasively and graciously.

You must pay for any wine or drinks with your meal, but that's **all the cash you will need** in the dining room. No tips are necessary until the end of the trip, when you may see fit to tip the dining room steward and the sommelier for their care and attention.

The menu for each meal will keep every palate satisfied and intrigued, and there may be open buffets at other times of the day (mid-afternoon for those who missed lunch and very late at night for those who have been socializing until the wee hours of the morning). If you have **special dietary needs** (kosher, low-salt, low-sugar, allergies), let the dining room steward know as soon as you arrive, and he will be glad to accommodate you.

Shipboard activities may range from the Captain's Dinner or evening gala to aerobics classes and game competitions. The ship will publish a daily calendar of events so that you will know when every meal is offered and what social, recreational, and entertainment activities are taking place that day.

HEALTH

Every floating passenger vessel is required to have a doctor on board, some will also have a number of nurses, and the largest ships have medical facilities more like a small hospital than an infirmary. There might be a small fee for a visit to the doctor's office, or you may be asked to pay only for any medicines that were dispensed, so bring along some money, just in case.

The ship's doctor will be available to treat most minor ailments, and in the event of a medical emergency will refer you to a specialist at the nearest port. Even if you never need to meet the shipboard physician, it's a comfort to know that qualified medical care is available.

Seasickness can afflict even the experienced ocean-goer. There's no need to suffer long: the ship's physician can give you a prescription to provide some relief.

Whatever else you may do when, or if, you get seasick, *don't drink* in an attempt to forget how rotten you feel. Drinking will only add to your instability, disorientation, and nausea. A good old-fashioned cure is to go out on deck for a few hours, breathe some fresh air, and gaze at the reason for your malaise until you get your sea legs and your stomach is calm.

Those who cruise in the winter months often get **badly sunburned.** Pack plenty in the way of sun lotions and sunscreens.

AT THE END OF THE VOYAGE

You are encouraged to tip those members of the ship's staff who have offered you help, advice, and cheerful, professional service. The cruise information brochure should mention a recommended tip for your cabin steward, dining room waiter, and busboy. To give you some idea of what is considered appropriate, the minimum tip for a cabin steward is $3 per person per day, for a dining room waiter or steward $3 per day for each person served, and for the busboy, $1 a day. Wine stewards or sommeliers and bartenders are tipped 15 percent of the cost of the wine or drinks you have ordered. Any person who gives you extraordinary service deserves a more generous tip, and a letter of commendation is always gratefully received.

As the end of the voyage nears, the cruise director will offer a session to the passengers on **debarkation procedures.** You should have found luggage tags and customs forms in your cabin by this time. You will attach these luggage tags to your bags and leave all but your carry-on luggage outside your door on the night before you arrive at the final port. Your steward will see that your baggage gets safely to the dock.

Customs should be little more than a formality at the end of the voyage. Keep all your receipts and pack your purchases near the top of your bags in the event that they must be inspected. Fill in your customs declaration forms as instructed by the cruise director and hand it to the customs official as your turn arrives. See Chapter 16 for information on customs duties. If you have any questions or fears, ask the cruise director or your cabin steward before you get to customs.

SPECIAL CRUISES

Cruise vacations or crossings are not limited to the young adult, able-bodied, married crowd. Cruising is open to practically anyone who has the desire and money to go, regardless of their marital status or age.

Many cruise lines encourage you to **bring along the kids** by offering incredibly low fares for children that accompany a full-paying adult. The best advice is to get a recommendation from a friend or travel agent for cruises that will be suitable to children and families. In the vernacular of the passenger ship industry "children" can be defined as any young person under the age of 12 or 14 or 17 — quite a range. Ask specifically if the cruise you have in mind is going to be right for *your* children — whether they are 4 and 6 or 15 and 17. Keep in mind that the cruise industry will probably only carry a full children's staff during the summer and school vacation periods.

Some cruises are better suited to families and children than others — the shorter cruises will be more attractive to children and are more likely to have a children's cruise director. Before you commit yourself to bringing the kids, check to be sure that the trip you have in mind offers a full calendar of children's events and will be sensitive to your child's needs and schedule.

The **singles crowd** is flocking to the "fun ships" not only because a cruise is a popular vacation, but also because there are opportunities to meet all kinds of other interesting people — single or not. Sadly, many cruise lines require single passengers to pay as much as double the fare for their cabin unless they can assign you another single roommate. The cruise lines that are known for their "fun ships" will cater to the singles crowd with good deals and imaginative bookings. Many lines will assign you another single roommate if you want to avoid the surcharge, and if you're lucky they won't be able to fill the space — at no extra cost to you.

As a single person you would probably enjoy the second sitting more (those at the second sitting are more likely to be adventurous and out-going). A table of eight or more will give you a chance to meet a number of different people right from the start.

A cruise vacation can be ideal for the **older or disabled traveler.** If you tell your travel agent of your needs, you and he or she will be able to come up with a ship and cruise that will be right for you. Newer ships have wider passageways, halls, and doorways, and will be more accessible to wheelchairs. Wheelchair passengers are asked to have an able-bodied person accompany them. Book a cabin on an upper deck near the elevators.

FREIGHTERS

Freighter travel is for the unhurried and the unimpatient. Some travel agents will be able to help you plan to book a trip as a passenger on a cargo vessel, but you will be better off contacting the shipping lines directly (addresses will be found in Chapter 23, "Useful Addresses").

The itinerary for a freighter is usually quite tentative in the early stages of the trip. All you may know for sure is the port you are departing from and where you hope to end up. It could take two weeks longer or shorter than anticipated, and you may stop at a dozen different ports along the way. Before you buy a ticket, try as best you can to get a complete itinerary. It is assumed that a passenger on a cargo ship is not in a great hurry to be anywhere, and that if the plans of the captain change along the way it won't make too much difference to you.

Most cargo ships don't carry any more than 12 passengers in addition to the officers and crew. You'll get to know the officers and crew well because you eat every meal with them, and may engage them in such recreational activities as cards, chess, backgammon, or other games. You will have to entertain yourself during the working day. Be sure you know how much time you have to explore while the ship is in port.

The passenger quarters on most freighters can be surprisingly spacious and comfortable. Be sure to pack a casual wardrobe that can be washed in the sink (there may be washing machines, but don't count on it) and hung to dry. Although you probably wouldn't use a travel clothesline on a cruise or crossing, you'll be glad to have one on a freighter voyage.

Passengers on a freighter pay by the day rather than a single sum in advance — probably because some passengers have been known to disembark at the strangest places. When you make your reservations you should ask what kind of a deposit will be necessary and how you should pay your fare if you're not definite on your destination. You can pay anywhere from $40 to more than $100 per day — considerably less than you would pay a cruise line. At those prices, and with all the incredible ports there are to visit, there is a freighter voyage for every budget and imagination.

Because the freighter's main function is to ship cargo, you will not have much in the way of shipboard entertainment. Life at sea can become tedious — be sure to pack reading and writing materials and portable games.

Because the passenger service on a freighter is much reduced from a cruise ship, you should tip 5 percent of your total fare divided equally between your stateroom and dining room steward on the last day of your trip. If you're on a longer voyage, tip weekly.

In some parts of the world you can go down to the harbor and ask around for a ship that's going where you want to go. This method of freighter travel is much less reliable than if you arrange your trip in advance, and you are traveling at your own risk. One of the authors and a friend once took a cargo ship from Barbados to Trinidad. After a raucous going-away party, the captain and the entire crew went to bed and the ship was steered through the night by only the deaf second mate, without benefit of radio or radar. Miraculously, the ship arrived safely in Port-of-Spain at dawn — but if it hadn't, the two passengers would have had no recourse.

CHAPTER NINE

GETTING AROUND

Most important, we feel, in navigating in an unfamiliar place, is
to orient yourself quickly. Purchase a map of the city or country ahead
of time and become familiar with it. Circle the places where you'll be.

DRIVING

The U.S. is ideal for car travel, the way Europe is ideal for
trains. In this country, take the back roads, away from the Interstate
Highway System. Try following one highway across the country — old
U.S. Route 66, or Highway 1 up the Atlantic Coast, or U.S. 2, which trav-
els west just south of and parallel to the Canadian border. (See also
Chapter 18, "Traveling with Children.")

Before deciding to drive abroad, remember that in a foreign
country a private car can be very isolating. Your reality is the interior of
the car, and the dynamics of your group, more than the culture of the
country. Gasoline is more expensive in most other countries than in the
U.S.A. You have to find a parking space. And you have to cope with
unfamiliar driving customs and traffic laws.

But a car does have the advantage of being your home away
from home. If you're on a tight budget you can combine transportation
and lodging costs by sleeping in your car at campgrounds. And you can
go wherever you want, whenever you want to.

In all Western European countries except Spain, Americans
can legally drive with just their own state driver's license. Spain and
many countries outside Western Europe require that visitors carry an
International Driving License. This can be obtained from any automobile

club affiliated with the American Automobile Association (you need not be a member). It costs $5.00.

We do not recommend renting a car in Asia, unless it's a Jeep in which you are going to tackle the Himalayas or other rugged areas. (Motorcycles make more sense, but are also more dangerous.) Few traffic jams can compare with the conglomeration of vehicles at a Calcutta crossroad — honking trucks, taxis, rickshaws, aggressive private cars, wagons drawn by water buffalos and horses, motorcycles, bicycles, pedestrians, and, always, the wild card — a holy cow wandering through. To make things more confusing, you must drive on the left.

For a list of questions to ask before renting a car, see Car Rental Checklist, Chapter 22.

Picnics are one of the pleasures of car travel. Get yourself some picnic equipment (see Chapter 11, "Dining"), and when you pass through a small town in late morning, purchase some fresh bread, local cheese, milk, cereal, tea or instant coffee, fruit, vegetables, cold cuts, nuts, yogurt, and dish soap. Or you can keep it simpler — one of us once hitchhiked through England and Wales, every day buying a loaf of local bread, some local cheese, and a little jar of mustard for a picnic. Every village offered its own unique product, and all were delicious.

If you have a **cooler** you'll be able to eat marvelously; if you have a stove you'll even be able to make a pot of tea in that nice spot you found off the side of the road with a view of Loch Lomond.

When you're **packing the car,** make sure you have available the things you'll need quickly. We would keep easily accessible a first-aid kit (see Chapter 4, "Health"), swimsuits, cameras, binoculars, sturdy walking shoes, and sweaters. All of these could be packed together in one duffel bag.

If you're only spending **one or two nights on the road,** pack a small bag with your overnight needs, so that you won't have to bring all of your luggage into your hotel or motel.

The less you can carry on top of your car, and the more inside it, the **more stable** the vehicle will be. Keep the center of gravity low by packing heavy items inside the car and light things on top.

You can **lease, rent, or buy a car in Europe** through Europe by Car, Inc., 1 Rockefeller Plaza, New York, NY 10020 (212-581-3040).

In order to **drive a new car** around Europe, you will need to know insurance requirements (the cost varies according to the make of car), and your car must carry a first-aid kit and have a "Danger" triangle on the back.

If you bring a new car back to the United States, you will have to prove that its **emission level** is acceptable by American standards.

Leasing can be cheaper than renting. There is usually a minimum period (two weeks or a month). If you lease a new car, you pay no mileage charge. After driving 1,000 kilometers, however, you must take the car in for service, which means you will be without the car for a day.

Small local rental agencies are cheaper than the big-name places. If you are willing to pick up your car somewhere other than the airport, you will save money. Some agencies actually provide shuttle service to and from the airport.

Some rental agencies in Europe will not rent cars to people **over 70 or under 25.**

When driving in another country, you must keep your wits about you — **car accidents** are the leading cause of death for travelers. The biggest challenge is driving on the left, as is the custom in a good part of the world (most countries that are or were part of the British Empire). Many travelers find shifting with the left hand most difficult. The clutch and the brake are in the same arrangement they are in American cars.

Allow at least a week to get accustomed to driving on the left. Be prepared, however, for lapses anytime in the first six months.

In many cities, both in this country and in other countries, you must stop the moment someone steps onto a **crosswalk** (called a "Zebra crossing" in England). If in doubt about local regulations, stop anyway. It is a much appreciated courtesy.

In much of Europe and the rest of the world, it seems as if the guiding principle is to drive as fast as possible at every opportunity, whether on a city street or on the famous Autobahn. Try to **drive slowly enough** so that you yourself can stay calm and collected.

The Autobahn is one of the world's most superb highways, well engineered and direct, but it has no speed limit. Beware — many tragic accidents occur on this highway.

In some European countries you must **prepay at the entrance** to the motorway (superhighway). Make sure you know your exit point before you arrive at the entrance toll booth. (If necessary, you can point out your route on your map to the toll booth attendant.)

If you haven't booked your hotel ahead of time, be sure to leave enough time at the **end of the day** to find lodging and a restaurant. Booking ahead is wise especially if you're traveling in high season or expecting to arrive very late. (See Chapter 10, "Lodging.")

When driving or taking public transportation, try to get into the habit of **thinking in kilometers,** if that's the standard measure in the country you're visiting. It's much more efficient than constantly converting. (In case you're forgotten, however, a kilometer is .62 of a mile.)

INTERNATIONAL HIGHWAY SIGNS

NO ENTRY

NO WAITING

NO U TURNS

SPEED LIMIT

(RIGHT) CURVE

INTERSECTION

DANGEROUS CURVES

RAILROAD CROSSING

TRAINS

One of us had the travel experience of her life when she rode fourth-class on a train across Brazil and Bolivia for a week. Instead of a swanky passenger car with seats and air conditioning, she and her friend and dozens of local passengers sat on the floor in boxcars, with the doors wide open to the rolling countryside, sleeping in sleeping bags at night and eating at the little stations. If you are young and hardy, you will never forget the experience of how local people travel long distances in Third World countries.

But you must stay alert, because certain amenities you might expect may be missing. When the author and her friend got off the above-mentioned train in one tiny station, the train started to leave without any whistle or announcement. She and her friend had to run and actually hop the train, assisted by many helping hands; otherwise they would have been left behind without their belongings.

In the United States, Amtrak offers very attractive family packages, comfortable trains, and scenic routes. Call 800-872-7245 for most current prices.

Eurailpass. For European travel, you must buy the Eurailpass in the United States — it is not available abroad. It is valid for Austria, Belgium, Denmark, Finland, France, Germany, Greece, Holland, Ireland, Italy, Luxembourg, Norway, Portugal, Spain, Sweden, and Switzerland. Note that although the pass is good for travel in Ireland, it is not valid in England, Scotland, or Wales — for those countries you must buy a BritRail Pass.

Obtain information on both passes from your travel agent, from Eurailpass, Box 325, Old Greenwich, CT 06870-0325, or from Forsyth Travel Library (see Chapter 23, "Useful Addresses").

A single **Eurailpass** will give you unlimited first-class rail travel. The ticket is also good for many scheduled boat trips on the Danube or the Rhine, steamers on Swiss lakes, and ferries between France and Ireland, Sweden and Denmark, and Greece and Italy. It is issued for 15 days, 21 days, or one, two, or three months. Children under 12 can obtain a Eurailpass for half the adult fare; children under 4 travel free on European trains.

The **Eurail Youthpass,** for people under 26, is issued for one to two months of unlimited second-class rail travel. At this writing, however, it is cheaper for children under 12 to travel on a half-fare Eurailpass.

The **Eurail Saverpass** is for a group of three or more persons traveling together (or a group of two or more from October through March). This pass is valid for 15 days of unlimited first-class rail travel. It's an excellent deal for adults traveling together, but for families it still can't match the value of the original Eurailpass.

The Eurailpass becomes valid on the first day you use it. You can get it stamped beforehand for the correct starting date, if you suspect you'll be in a hurry when you get to the station. Be sure to get the stamp before you board the train; otherwise you may pay a penalty.

Once your pass is stamped, you can simply board the train and flash the pass.

Do not purchase a Eurailpass if you are going to take a train to one place and stay there. The pass is for travelers who want to cover a lot of territory in a limited time.

The Eurailpass also entitles the holder to reduced rates for car rentals in France, reduced fares on some Europabus lines in Belgium, France, Italy and Switzerland, and free passage on trains between certain airports and cities (Amsterdam, Barcelona, Brussels, Dusseldorf, Frankfurt, Paris, and Zurich).

Even with a Eurailpass, you must secure a reservation in advance if you want to be sure of getting a seat. A reservation is compulsory for travel in sleepers. In Spain, you must have a reservation or you will not be allowed to board an express train. You may also reserve a seat in the dining car.

If all of your train travel will be done in one country, find out whether there may be a **cheaper pass** just for that country. A Swiss Holiday Card, for example, is at this writing a little more than half the cost of a Eurailpass for 15 days. Contact the Forsyth Travel Library (see Chapter 23, "Useful Addresses").

There are special train pass discounts available for **students and seniors,** if you make arrangements through a recognized organization such as the Council on International Educational Exchange, the International Youth Hostel Organization, or the American Association of Retired Persons. (See Chapter 23, "Useful Addresses," for addresses.) Have your membership card with you.

You'll save money on lodging if you **travel at night.** Reserve a berth and you'll get both your transportation and your bed for one price. Inquire when you make your reservation whether you must also reserve a meal.

In Europe, a **sleeper** is a bedroom, and a **couchette** is an open bunk (with pillow and blanket but no privacy). The price of the sleeper varies according to type of accommodation and distance traveled; for the couchette you pay a flat charge per night.

Bring a **blanket or extra sweaters** for night train travel, especially in the spring or fall. In winter, train cars can be stiflingly hot.

Bring a **picnic basket** or lunchbox for the kids. In many countries, vendors will appear at the windows during station stops and offer snacks for sale. In Third World countries this can be a thriving business. You will be offered local delicacies and a cup of sweet tea or coffee through the train window.

Have extra soap, a towel, and toilet paper with you and accessible if you are **traveling for a few days** on a train.

If you've reserved a seat, be sure to sit in the **correct seat in the correct car!** Otherwise your car may be shunted off to a different city — or country.

When the conductor stamps your ticket, **examine it** to make sure the correct portion has been taken. Keep your ticket; in some cities and countries you will need it when you get off.

TRAIN STATIONS

When you arrive at the station, always look immediately for the poster or computerized timetable showing you which track your train is at.

Most European train stations have a **diagram of each train** showing the location of each car, so that you will know exactly where on the platform to stand. Look also for "pictograms" showing where to find restaurants, rest rooms, baggage areas, etc.

Throughout the world, many terminals have a **"Left Luggage" storage facility.** If you can find such a service you will be free of your luggage for some sightseeing. Make sure you retrieve the luggage in plenty of time for your departure. These are popular services and if you're late you can face a long line of anxious travelers and cross clerks.

Some European stations will **forward your luggage** to meet you at the train station in another city, thus freeing you to travel unencumbered. This usually takes a few days. Some stations can send your bags from the station to the airport, and, in Switzerland, even onto your plane.

BUSES

Buses can be exhausting, but they are the cheapest form of motorized transportation and one of the very best ways to penetrate a country. In some parts of the world buses are packed to the gills with people and then careen up mountain passes and over suspension bridges with the radio blasting and the horn honking. In other countries they are comfortable, air-conditioned, serene. In all kinds of buses, you will have an excellent opportunity to meet people.

In the United States, Greyhound and Trailways both offer reduced fares, sightseeing packages, and special passes. See Chapter 23, "Useful Addresses."

On American buses children under five travel free; from six to eleven years old they ride for half fare. There are special rates available for disabled travelers, clergy, members of the armed forces, and groups.

In London and Paris you can prebook unlimited subway and city bus travel vouchers along with rail travel bargains.

BOATS

We recommend taking a boat wherever possible — through the canals of Bangkok or Venice or Southern France, up the west coast of Canada to Alaska, across the English Channel, around Boston Harbor. Cities seem to look their best and make most sense when seen from the water.

The Eurailpass and its offshoots will cover many types of boat trips in Europe, including steamers and ferries.

GETTING AROUND IN A CITY

Use your city map to plan your route to places you want to see. A tourist office will usually have a map of the city bus or subway system.

If the language is unfamiliar to you, have the hotel desk clerk write on a piece of paper the name of your hotel. If you get lost or disoriented, you can simply show the slip of paper to a cab driver and be taken back to your room or hotel without too much trouble.

Even if you plan to stroll around an unfamiliar city, consider taking an **orientation tour** your first day there. It will point out places of interest, give you an idea of layout and neighborhoods, and provide some interesting background and history. Then when you're ready to negotiate the city by yourself, you'll have some sense of distances and routes.

In some European cities, city buses and subways run on an **honor system**. You buy a ticket, board the bus, and punch your own ticket. No one checks, but there are serious penalties for people found with unpunched tickets. In the Lyons, France, métro, for example, random checks are made, and those without tickets are punished.

Certain seats on public transport are reserved for pregnant women, war veterans, and disabled people. Usually there is a sign to indicate this. If people are standing and there's an empty seat, don't assume they knew you were coming! Check for a sign indicating restricted use.

WALKING

Trek in India or Nepal, hill-walk in Scotland, amble through the Alps, walk from village to village in South America, prowl Paris or London.... Walking is without doubt the finest way to travel if you're strong and have time, especially in the Third World where you will have a lot of interesting company. In India, one of us and her companion walked for a week through the Himalayas with a *sadhu* (holy man), and her images of those dramatic mountains are forever brightened by the memory of his warm humor and resourcefulness.

Have a good map, a pair of sturdy, well-broken-in walking shoes, extra pairs of cotton socks, and as light a pack as possible. Dress in layers, so that you can strip down as the day warms up. It's very soothing to bathe your feet and change into a fresh pair of socks if you should come upon a stream or well at midday.

Bring a poncho that covers you and your knapsack, and if you are wearing sneakers, have with you some rubber galoshes that you can put on over them if you're walking in the rain. There's nothing so uncomfortable as sloshing along in wet sneakers — unless it's putting them on again the next morning.

Have a good breakfast in the morning before you set out, and bring with you some trail food ("gorp") and a canteen for a mid-morning break. We think it's particularly nice to stop at a grocery to buy a picnic lunch, and then walk on to another village for supper and sleep.

Don't overestimate how far you can go. Although humans are technically capable of walking three miles an hour, we have found walking twenty miles in one day with a pack to be quite arduous, especially over hills. Be conservative in your estimates and you'll have time to relax.

GOING BY BIKE

People do not often consider the bicycle as a mode of transportation either here or abroad. It is true that you need to be in good physical condition, and that you can pack only as much as you can carry in specially made bicycle bags. But if you really want to see the countryside and meet the locals along the way, going by bike will provide the greatest opportunities.

You will need to own or rent a bike that is in good working condition. If you rent one, be sure to select a bike that is right for your height and weight: there should be enough air in the tires to withstand the weight of you and your fully packed bags, and you should just be able to touch the ground with the tip of your toe when you sit on the seat.

As far as physical preparation is concerned, you should take a good ride (of about ten miles) five days a week for at least three weeks prior to your departure.

Transporting your bike by air or rail need not be a hassle. Airlines will accept it as one item of your luggage. If you are going by air, try to obtain a box from a local bike shop. (These are becoming harder to find, however, because new bikes are now being shipped wrapped in many layers of heavy plastic.)

If you can't find a box, make yourself a "bike bag" that looks like a big envelope for your bicycle. It should accommodate the bike with its front wheel removed, have a big flap on the outside, and have either an inside pocket for the front wheel or a length of fabric in which to wrap it. Sew on a handle or shoulder strap, and you'll be all set. We recommend using a fabric such as parachute cloth, which will fold easily and not take up much space. All you'll need to secure your bike bag is some rope or some packing tape, a roll of which you can bring along.

Cyclists abroad do not feel nearly as threatened by drivers as they do at home. Bicyclists are a common sight in almost every foreign country, and those who travel by bike are generally treated with respect and care.

HITCHHIKING

At its best, hitchhiking is much more than just a way to get to your destination free. It can bring great rewards — long-lasting friendships and marvelous experiences. It lets you into people's lives and gives special insights into and memories of the area you're visiting.

But hitchhiking is also extremely risky. Hitchhikers must be very cautious and alert. They must be good at judging character, fast. They must be courteous and friendly, so that the driver is glad he picked

HITCHHIKING TIPS

■ Never hitchhike at night.

■ Study a map and learn every detail of your route — town names, highway route numbers, distances, landmarks. Carry your map, folded to show the correct region, in an accessible pocket of your luggage, and keep it near you to refer to while you're in the car.

■ Know the laws regarding hitchhiking in the country you're visiting. It is nearly always forbidden (not to mention extremely dangerous) to hitchhike on a limited-access multi-lane highway. Stay on entrance ramps — or avoid high-speed highways entirely.

■ On secondary roads, stand where you can be seen from at least 200 feet away, and where there is plenty of room for the car or truck to pull safely off the road. Intersections are ideal because the traffic slows down.

■ The early hitcher gets the ride — get out there at dawn!

■ Take a city bus or subway to the outskirts of town to pick up your highway.

■ If there is a line of hitchhikers, go to the end of it.

■ Make sure you and your belongings are safely off the road.

■ Use the right signal! Notice what others do.

■ Dress neatly and modestly. Wearing outlandish clothes is asking for trouble.

■ Do not smoke cigarettes or sit while hitchhiking.

■ Before you get into a car, ask the driver where he's going. Take a good look at him and any other occupants of the car. If you don't like the looks of the ride, simply and courteously refuse it.

■ Do not accept a ride with two or more men, unless you are absolutely certain the situation is safe.

■ The safest rides are with women, couples, families, and solo men. (Solo men are by far the most likely to pick you up.)

■ Wear your seatbelt in the car.

■ Keep your belongings next to you in the car, just in case you have to get out.

■ Do not fall asleep in the car.

■ If you begin to feel uncomfortable with the driver, ask to stop at the next service station. Say you feel carsick. Once you have stopped, take your belongings out of the car and inform the driver that you will not be going any farther.

them up, yet they must never be flirtatious. They must be able to talk their way out of difficult situations. And they must know exactly where they are going.

Certain places, such as Canada and Northern Europe, are considered safer for hitchhiking than others. The United States is not a safe place to hitchhike, nor is Southern Europe.

One woman alone will get a ride quickly but will continually find herself in tense or dangerous situations. Two men will find hitching together safe but very slow. The best combination for hitchhiking is a couple. Couples seem to project a certain normalcy and wholesomeness that attract drivers with the same qualities.

Talk to other hitchhikers about best routes, best places to stay, best "hitching posts." Some cities or routes are notoriously bad places to get a ride. The Sudbury/Sault Ste.-Marie area of Ontario is one such spot; Tok Junction, Alaska is another. We've heard of a man and a woman, traveling separately, who got stuck in Tok Junction together for two weeks and ended up getting legally hitched — married! If you don't have that degree of flexibility, find out about such places and avoid them by taking a different route or waiting for a ride that goes beyond.

Think through exactly what you would do in an emergency. Women traveling together sometimes select a code word so that one can alert the other if she senses a problem.

Don't use a sign stating your destination unless you want one ride on a superhighway all the way into a big city. Otherwise, a sign may commit you to a ride you don't like the looks of. Also, you will forfeit the interesting local traffic.

CHAPTER TEN

LODGING

(See also Hotel Reservation Checklist, Chapter 22.)

Hotels may eat up a larger piece of your budget than any other single expense (unless you are going to Asia, where the plane ticket is expensive and lodging is cheap). If you are traveling in foreign countries, book ahead only your first night's reservation. Once you're over there, you can find the smaller places. Small neighborhood hotels are not only inexpensive, but they also offer a truer sense of the place. In this country, on the other hand, it works better to reserve ahead, using a guidebook or budget motel guide.

Help in finding lodging is perhaps the single most valuable function of guidebooks. Not only do they list address, telephone, and price range, along with a brief description of facilities and ambience, but their endorsement counts as a recommendation (*not* a guarantee) that the place is honest and clean.

You may find, however, that you meet the same tourists over and over again — obviously they have the same criteria you do and they are picking out the same hotels from the same book. To avoid feeling like part of a herd, pick up more than one guidebook. Cut out the relevant portions and bring them along, not the entire bound books. You can toss them out as you leave the country, or hand them to an incoming tourist.

Before going to less touristed areas of the world, such as South America, Africa, and the South Pacific, you may wish to avail yourself of **all available guidebooks,** to give yourself the maximum amount of pre-information. Guidebooks are invariably excellent reading.

If you are traveling without a guidebook, or you find yourself in a town it doesn't cover, here are some pointers on finding a hotel.

■ Ask other travelers for their recommendations. They may tell you the place you're heading for that night has bedbugs, or excellent coffee, or that there's a better, cheaper place around the corner.

■ If we're staying in a city for more than just a night or two, we may stay in one place, perhaps a hotel, the first night, and then stroll around the city the first day looking for a more appropriate place — cheaper or more luxurious, more in the center or closer to the beach.

■ In a beach city, such as Mazatlan, Mexico, a hotel on the beach may be astoundingly expensive, but one just a block away could fall within your means.

■ Always ask to see the room before you take it. (In many countries, this is standard.) Make sure it is clean, well equipped, and located in a satisfactory and safe part of the hotel. Check to see that heat and/or air conditioning actually work, that windows open and close, or, if you're in the tropics, that there are window screens. Make sure doors and windows lock. Listen to the street noise level. If you aren't happy with the room, ask to see another one — or ask that the price be reduced.

Check to see where the **fire escape** is and what the fire regulations are. They should be posted on the back of the door in the room. (See also Chapter 15, "Safety and Security.")

European hotels often have a variety of **room and bath** options. The top of the line is the bedroom with an attached bath and toilet. If you ask for a bed and bath you may get a bedroom with a shower stall, with the toilet down the hall, so if you want a toilet in your room you must ask for it. Bathrooms in older European hotels often do not include a toilet. (If you are looking for a toilet, don't be polite and ask for bathroom — that may be all you get!)

If a hotel has a feature you simply love, such as a nice view from your window or a pleasant courtyard to sit in, take it. That's what good memories are made of — but remember that that's also what eats up your money.

You will have the best luck if you look for and decide on your hotel in the **late morning or early afternoon.** Leave your luggage with the concierge or room clerk and you can go out and enjoy yourself for the rest of the day.

If you're arriving late, and you haven't booked ahead, try to give yourself time at the end of the day to find a hotel before you're desperate with fatigue. In looking for a hotel, we make a point of checking out three places before committing to any. The most visible hotel is usually not the cheapest.

But if you arrive in late evening you may also be able to negotiate the price of a room, since the hotel may prefer having the room occupied for a lower price than having the room empty.

In Asia, at major transportation terminals, you'll be surrounded by **taxi drivers** urging you to go with them to one hotel or another. They are paid by the hotel. We have had good luck in sizing up one driver who looked decent and honest, and letting him take us to his hotel. Make sure the hotel will be where you want to be — downtown, for example, or near the train station.

If you are a budget traveler, look for the friendly **neighborhood hotel** that caters to locals, not the fancy place that caters to tourists. For instance, in Paris, a friend of ours recently found a clean, respectable hotel in a lovely old part of town for $10 a night — and had several to choose from — by simply walking around and inquiring at neighborhood hotels instead of at obvious tourist places.

When you accept the room, ask what the **exact price** will be, including tax and service charge, so that you will know what to expect on the bill. Have the desk clerk or concierge write down the figure.

Your concierge is many things — guardian of your privacy and safety, hailer of taxis, fountain of information about bus routes, good restaurants, theater tickets, reliable doctors, and pharmacies with all-night hours, and in general your link to the world you are visiting.

Breakfast in continental Europe ("Continental Breakfast") is a cup of coffee with hot milk and a roll with jam and butter. In Great Britain and Ireland, on the other hand, breakfast is enormous — juice, cereal, eggs, bacon or ham or both, racks of toast, crumpets or scones, jam, marmalade, cakes, and pots of tea.

Pension complet and *Demi-pension* are an especially good deal in a two-star hotel with a three-star restaurant. The price includes your lodging and food for one day. You'll be tempted to stay forever! *Pension complet* includes a continental breakfast, lunch (often a large one), and dinner. Usually you eat the fixed menu or plate of the day with few or no choices.

Demi-pension includes a continental breakfast and one other meal, usually dinner. This is a good choice for those who wish to tour or hike during the day, but return to the hotel in the evening.

The American Plan means you get a big "American breakfast," lunch, and dinner included in the price of your lodging; the Modified American Plan (M.A.P.) means just breakfast.

A restaurant in the hotel is convenient, but does raise the price. If you're on a budget, look for a hotel without a restaurant and ask the desk clerk or concierge to recommend a nearby eating place.

Check with the national tourist office or city tourist office for a **lodging reservation service.** In many countries these are highly efficient. In Great Britain and Ireland, for example, you can arrive in a city, go to the office of the National Tourist Board (always conveniently located), and book a room at a local B & B. We've done this even at 11:00 at night, although that's risky at the height of the season.

Or you can book a room ahead of time in the city you expect to reach that evening. Give your estimated time of arrival so that they don't give your room away if you arrive after supper. Then you can travel to your destination in a carefree and leisurely way.

IN THE UNITED STATES

In this country, unlike Europe, a guide to budget motels, bed and breakfast places or campgrounds will save you a lot of money and time, especially if you're traveling with your family. Plan your route ahead of time, and make your reservations. This is far more reliable than trying to find an inexpensive motel at the end of the day. It also helps you to budget your lodging costs in advance.

In the U.S. and Canada, as in cities throughout the world, **YMCA's and YWCA's** are safe, clean and reliable. Many offer family accommodations and have recreational facilities, such as gyms and pools. Canadian Y's are an excellent value.

To reserve a room, send the Y a postcard with your expected date of arrival. This may not hold your room under pressure, but it can help.

If you stay at a hotel chain, you can make all your reservations at once.

HOSTELS

Hostels are not only for young people. The International Youth Federations now has a card that affords a discount to people over 59. Get a copy of the *International Youth Hostel Handbook* (different volumes cover different areas of the world) for specific addresses and facilities. Write AYH, P.O. Box 37613, Washington, DC 20013-7613 for membership card.

Hostels are reliable, cheap, clean, safe, and fun. They also have certain rules. You must carry your membership card. Men sleep in one dormitory and women in another (although some hostels have a few rooms for couples or families). The doors may be locked as early as 10 p.m. (a few stay open till midnight). There is a maximum number of days you can stay, and usually you are not allowed to hang around during the day.

A hostel may serve communal meals or it may have a kitchen, equipped with utensils, for you to use (you must clean up after yourself).

Hostels are ideal for solo travelers — you will have other people to talk to and you might meet another single you'd like to travel with. In this country and abroad, you will meet people from all over the world.

The original purpose of hostels was to serve people who are roughing it — hiking or bicycling. Thus they are located in scenic areas, not necessarily convenient to the city center.

Arrive when the hostel opens in the afternoon, to assure yourself of a bed. You will need to have your own towel, soap, and sheet. A sleeping sack is often recommended — just fold a single flat sheet lengthwise and stitch around one short end and the long side.

OTHER ACCOMMODATIONS

Staying in castles is a very special experience — exciting for children, romantic for couples. You will need reservations; use your guidebook or inquire at a national tourist bureau.

You can also choose from farmhouse accommodations, canal boats, abbeys, and private homes.

Why not rent a villa? Especially if you have children, this is a delightful way to visit France, Italy, Portugal, Spain, Malta, or Greece. Friends of ours rented a lovely villa for a month in Spain through At Home Abroad, Inc. (405 East 56th St., New York, NY 10022).

Camping is very popular in Europe. Invest in the National Camper Association "carnet," a card that can get you a discount to many campgrounds throughout the world. Reserve a space ahead of time.

For information on rentals all over the world, read the classified ads in the International Herald Tribune or in local foreign papers. See also Chapter 20, "Time Sharing."

If you are traveling on a budget in South or Central America, be sure to buy a **hammock.** You 'll use it in beach cabañas, on river boats, and even in cheap hotel rooms.

CHAPTER ELEVEN

DINING

We recommend that if you are going to splurge on anything, it be on food. Whether it's a new fruit in South America or a new wine in France, raw fish at a Japanese *sushi-ya* or fish and chips by a London dock, discovering new foods is one of the great pleasures of and reasons for traveling.

If you'll be in a country where English isn't spoken, read up on the cuisine ahead of time so that you won't be totally ignorant of the country's specialties. Purchase a phrasebook before you go and study the section on reading menus. The *Berlitz Guide to Latin American Spanish for Travelers,* for example, has a substantial section on menus, with a page devoted to each of a dozen courses — and it makes a few recommendations as well! (Don't worry about looking like a tourist with a phrasebook. Your concern is with having a delicious meal.)

Most guidebooks will also include pointers for negotiating a foreign menu. If you don't want to take the entire book into the restaurant, just clip and staple the relevant section and carry it in your pocket or handbag.

Ask for your waiter's recommendation. And be adventurous! Don't order the same dish everywhere you go — try something new.

In many parts of the world the **midday meal** is the main meal of the day, after a skimpy continental breakfast. In Great Britain and Ireland, though, both breakfast and the midday meal tend to be hearty, especially in rural areas, followed by a light "tea" at suppertime and another "tea" (usually sweet breads and cakes) just before bed.

If you're driving, carry **picnic supplies** with you. Wash up your dishes at a rest area if there was no running water at your picnic site. Have with you a couple of dish towels, a small cutting board, a good knife, can and bottle openers, a cup for each person, a thermos, a roll of plastic bags, and a roll of paper towels. Paper products are hard to find outside the U.S. and Canada; invest in a set of plates and flatware, and some sort of container to keep everything in. It goes without saying that you should take with you, when you leave, any trash your picnic generates.

Ask at the **city tourist office** for information on restaurants. Also use your guidebook, and ask your concierge or hotel desk clerk for recommendations.

In many parts of the world, **everything closes down** from noon till about two p.m. for lunch. Restaurants often cater to this by serving an inexpensive full meal. If you are on a budget, this is the time to eat your big meal of the day.

Many restaurants also have a fixed meal — one or two choices of appetizer, a salad, main course, one or two choices of dessert — which might in France be called "Le Menu" or "Le Plat du Jour" (the menu in France is "la carte," which can be confusing!). This is always the best deal for the money, and the freshest food.

You'll save money if you can break the three-main-meals-a-day habit, and have a light lunch or a light supper.

KEEPING RESTAURANTS WITHIN YOUR MEANS

■ Read the menu before you sit down (it's usually posted, in this country, Europe, and Asia).

■ Look for smorgasbords, buffets, salad bars, other "all you can eat" situations, and have this be the big meal of the day.

■ Choose the special of the day.

■ Order a complete dinner, not individual items a la carte.

■ When in Europe, Canada, and the U.S., patronize Asian restaurants.

■ For health as well as economy, eat vegetarian.

In many parts of the world, silverware is not a part of the mealtime scene. **Chopsticks,** used throughout East Asia, do not take long to master if you keep at it and don't get embarrassed by your first fumblings.

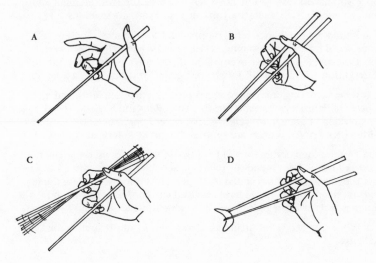

A. Hold one chopstick in the U-shaped area between thumb and index finger, and rest the lower end on the tip of your ring finger.

B. Hold the other chopstick with thumb, index finger, and middle finger, as if it were a pencil.

C. Manipulate upper chopstick, using thumb as pivot.

D. Enjoy!

Eating with one's fingers, as is done throughout South Asia, is traumatic for the western visitor. In restaurants, forks and spoons will be provided, but private homes usually lack them. We traveled with a mess kit fork and spoon — until we sat down to a meal in a lovely home among gracious friends who were eating with their fingers, and we couldn't bring ourselves to pull out the utensils. Remember to eat with your right hand as Asians do (although Asians have come to accept western quirks). They customarily use the left hand for all unsanitary tasks and the right hand for eating. You may not be given a napkin, but you will probably be given a finger bowl in which to dip your fingers after the meal.

DINING IN FRANCE

There are special traditions associated with dining out in France. Eating fine French food in a good restaurant is an experience not to be missed, and we recommend it as a very special occasion to splurge, even if you are traveling with children.

■ Remember that you must call a good restaurant for a reservation. Once you have a reservation, however, you have the table all night and you can concentrate totally on your meal and your companions.

■ Restaurants in France tend to open later for dinner — 7:30 or so. Since you'll be there all evening, service can be leisurely. After dessert, you are expected to linger over coffee. If you don't ask for your bill ("L'addition, s'il vous plaît!") with your coffee, you may have a long wait.

■ When ordering, ask your waiter's recommendation. More and more waiters in Parisian restaurants are able to understand English. You should try speaking in French, as well; we have never experienced the surliness with which French waiters are supposed to greet American French.

■ Tips are included in the bill (but not in the prices on the menu) in most of France. Most menus or bills say "Service Compris," which means that the management has added in 15 percent somewhere along the line and you need not tip. If you have received extraordinary service, however, you may leave a "pour boire" — a little something for a drink.

■ Where service is not included, 15 percent is standard, as in the United States.

In Europe, people tend to hold their **fork in their left hand** and their knife in the right, to eliminate the awkwardness of switching utensils back and forth. We have found this an easy and graceful habit to pick up.

Eat yogurt to **cool your palate** after a meal that's highly spiced with chili peppers or hot curries. Or do what the Mexicans do — eat *more* hot food.

TIPPING

In most areas of the world, it is expected that a customer will leave a gratuity, or tip, to those who provide you with service. The practice of tipping varies from country to country, and can add confusion to an already foreign situation. If you tip someone for service in a foreign country, keep the following points in mind:

■ As a general rule, 10 to 15 percent of the net bill constitutes a reasonable tip for all kinds of service.

■ Check to be sure that your bill does not already include a tip ("Service Compris"). In this case, an additional tip is unnecessary.

■ Porters are tipped according to the number of bags they are handling for you.

■ Barbers and hairdressers are tipped 10 to 15 percent of the net bill.

■ In some countries, doormen and ushers are tipped; find out what local custom dictates.

■ Wine stewards (or sommeliers) are usually tipped 10 percent of the cost of the wine.

■ Tour guides and leaders and bus drivers should be tipped.

■ Observe the local customs. Tipping is strongly discouraged in China, the Soviet Union, Samoa, Tahiti, and Tonga. It is not generally practiced in Scandinavia, Switzerland, the Netherlands, parts of Asia and Southeast Asia, as well as a few countries on the southern Africa continent.

■ If you received especially good service, be sure that you hand-deliver your tip to the person. More often than not, those who take and profit from your tip are not the people who have earned it.

■ Don't allow yourself to be bullied into overtipping. Don't go above 15 percent or you make it harder for the next tourist.

■ Above all, use your instinct. If service is good, acknowledge it in your tip.

If you'd like to know more about tipping customs in foreign countries, write to the International Federation of Women's Travel Organizations (IFWTO) for a handy little pamphlet on tipping (See Chapter 23, "Useful Addresses").

CHAPTER TWELVE

ENJOYING YOURSELF

The pleasure of traveling begins in the planning, as you write to tourist offices for materials and browse through newspapers for discount fares and interesting places to go. All too often the departure date sneaks up on you and you have to rush madly to get everything done. (See Chapter 22 for a checklist of what to do before you go.)

We suspect you won't need much advice on how to enjoy yourself while traveling, but here are a few suggestions that have helped us in the past.

Get up at or before dawn. Seeing how the day begins lets you *in* to an unfamiliar place, whether it's hearing the roosters crow in the West Indies or observing the bicycle rush hour in Beijing. One of us remembers the beautiful city of Quito, Ecuador, slowly coming to life before dawn as market vendors streamed in from the villages to set up their booths, carrying huge bundles of fruits and vegetables on their backs or on donkeys. Certain places are truly sublime at dawn — the Grand Canyon, for example, or the Taj Mahal — and you probably won't be sharing them with other tourists!

Take different forms of transportation. You can ride a camel to see the Pyramids, take a skiing tour through Norway or ride horseback through Outer Mongolia. Ask your travel agent.

In particular, **take boats.** You can take boats through the canals of Amsterdam, Bangkok and, of course, Venice. You can rent canal boats in France or England. You can take steamers up the Rhine or the Danube past romantic castles, take the Circle Tour of New York City, or

109

take swan boats in Boston's Public Garden. Eurailpass covers ferries between many European countries; it will cover most of the cost of the boat from Corfu, Greece across the Adriatic to Brindisi, Italy.

Kids and adults often have a prejudice against **museums,** but a good museum can be immensely exciting. The small museum of the Grand Canyon, the Whaling Museum on Nantucket Island, the museum at Omaha Beach in Normandy — these are places children will never forget.

A friend who knows and loves France tells us that older French people still remember and honor Americans who served in the **Second World War.** If you are a veteran, or your parents were veterans, you will be warmly received. Be sure to let the local people know if you are on a pilgrimage back to towns where you stayed or fought during the war. There are a number of war memorials and museums honoring those who served.

Find out what **events are taking place** while you're visiting. Every area has its own specialty that's featured in a festival. There are festivals celebrating corn and rhubarb in South Dakota, maple syrup in Vermont, zucchini in New Hampshire, tobacco in Kentucky, and oysters in Lousiana.

Don't forget **town, county, and state fairs,** which take place in the summer and fall. County fairs are our favorite — large enough to be exciting, but not too sophisticated. We recommend the Dutchess County Fair in Rhinebeck, New York, for wonderful food and atmosphere.

Walk. Whether you're in San Francisco or the Himalayas, walking will give you a flavor of the place you can't get enclosed in a vehicle. It helps you to know where you are — and it's good for you besides.

Talk to people, in their own language, if possible.

If you find you constantly meet the same Americans over and over, it means you probably have the same guidebook. Often Americans are embarrassed at seeing others of their own nationality. We recommend that you **make friends** with the people you keep running into — you and they evidently have the same taste and the same traveling style, and probably have a great deal in common. You'll get the most useful tips of all from your fellow travelers.

Be sensitive to **local customs.** The more different the culture you're visiting is, the likelier it is to have certain customs you'd never guess you mustn't violate. Often there is a certain protocol associated with religion — you must slip out of your shoes to enter a Moslem, Hindu, Sikh, or Buddhist shrine, but you must put on a hat to enter certain churches. Women are not supposed to sit next to Buddhist monks (on public transportation, for example). You must rely on your guidebook for this kind of information.

If you're on a **package tour,** you can enhance your enjoyment by advance preparation — knowing exactly where the tour takes you and reading up on the background of the places. Collect addresses of people you can drop in on. Make the most of your free time.

Above all, **be adventurous.** Remember that the great travel experiences belong to those who are ready for them. One of the authors was once on an ancient public bus, toiling up the dizzying heights of the Himalayas. Her fear of heights was so strong that she had her eyes closed most of the time. Her husband, meanwhile, was gazing out over spectacular vistas, seeing from an eagle's perspective endless mountain ranges stretching out. His wise suggestion to her was to feel the fear, but to keep looking anyway — not to miss one of the greatest sights a human being could see. Be cautious, be careful, but don't let that interfere with enjoying the magnificent adventure of travel.

MEETING PEOPLE

The warmest memories of your trip will undoubtedly involve the new friends you've made. Whether these are natives or tourists like yourself, they will make your trip more special and meaningful, and some may become lifelong friends.

Some countries are easier to meet people in than others. Where tourists are rarely seen, you'll frequently find yourself surrounded by interested natives, and you'll often be invited for tea and a chat. In other countries, people might be reluctant to invade your privacy. Men in particular tend to have difficulty meeting local women abroad.

Despite the stereotype of the "ugly American," most people do in fact want to meet Americans.

First and foremost, before you leave home, gather from your friends at home the addresses of *their* friends living abroad. This is the best way to enter into the life of the country you're visiting, to experience the way people live — and to sample home cooking! It is also a good safeguard should you need legal or medical help in a foreign country. You can write a note in advance of your trip, or have your American friends do so, or you can drop a line when you're in the vicinity. Offer to bring a present or photographs from your American friends. The people you visit may then send you to their friends, until you have a network of acquaintances around the country.

Bring little gifts of your own for the people listed in your address book. Easy-to-carry but much appreciated presents include T-shirts, lighters, novel pens, little flashlights, baseball caps, and scarves. Bluejeans and denim jackets take up more room in your suitcase but are greatly appreciated by teenagers.

In Northern Europe, where the locals tend to respect your privacy, the best place by far to meet people is in the local pub. Most pubs attract both sexes and all ages, and the atmosphere is warm and congenial. Your new acquaintances will buy you drinks; etiquette demands that you "stand a round" yourself. If you don't drink, just substitute a soft drink.

Traveling in a rented car can be isolating. Take public transportation instead. Local buses are always a memorable experience.

Trains are classic places to meet people. Conversations are struck up effortlessly in train compartments and may result in exchanged addresses and lifelong friendships.

To meet fellow travelers, the American Express office or the American Embassy — wherever you receive your mail — is a natural place.

When you take pictures of a local, you might offer or be asked to send a copy to your subject. This can lead to a long-term correspondence.

For recreation, do as the locals do. Go to football games, flea markets, fairs, and festivals.

Attend religious services! You will be surrounded by people at the end of the service. Remember that there are customs governing dress in churches, temples, and synagogues.

LANGUAGE

Not only will you get around better if you try to speak the language, but you'll also make more friends. People everywhere appreciate your effort to communicate on their terms, and many deeply resent the American who assumes everyone speaks English.

Learning a language is easiest when you're immersed in it, surrounded by native speakers. You'll have exact pronunciations to imitate, and you'll tune in to the flowing rhythms of speech. Even if you could never pass French 101, you'll find you're picking up the language now.

A few months before departure, purchase an instructional language cassette. Play it regularly to get the sound of the language in your ears. Keep it on while you pack your suitcase.

Pick up a small paperback dictionary of the language and a pocket phrasebook. Phrasebooks are useful for specific situations, but a dictionary will help you really learn the language.

Key to learning a language, as with many skills, is a **lack of embarrassment.** You can't learn a new language without making mistakes — if the fear of making errors keeps you from practicing, then you'll never be able to speak fluently.

It is as easy to learn **three or four related words** at once as it is to learn one. Choose a few words that might be used together — to walk, to look for, to see.

The *Gimmick* books by Adrienne (New York: W. W. Norton, 1977) use this technique in teaching you colloquial Spanish, French, German, or Italian.

If you'll be **off the beaten path** it's more crucial to have a smattering of the language. If you're in a country with a different alphabet than ours, become as familiar as possible with the letters so that you can make out the road signs.

Note that in many countries there is both an **informal and a formal way of saying "you."** To learn when each form is appropriate takes time, and comes as you get to know the particular culture. In French, for example, the formal *vous* is expected when you first meet people. When you hear them start using *"tu"* in addressing you, then you may do the same. Many people older than 60, however, are more formal, and will continue to use the *vous* form even after you have come to know them quite well. Don't feel insulted — they may use the *tu* form only with their immediate families. If you are young, on the other hand, young people may never use the *vous* form with you. Take your lead from the people you're with, but if in doubt use *vous*.

In Spanish, it is more likely that you will be addressed by a contemporary as *"tu,"* instead of *"usted,"* even when you first meet. Again, listen carefully. When addressing an older person, always use the polite form.

If you'll be in one country for a while, why not attend language classes or **hire a tutor?** The formal instruction will help make sense of the language you hear all around you.

With a tutor the price will vary according to his or her age and experience. You do not necessarily need an expert teacher, just a native speaker. Your tutor may become an important resource for you — a man who tutored one of the authors in Hindi in India ended up becoming a good friend, taking her and her husband to weddings, political events, and family occasions, and even taught them to cook Indian style.

You can purchase **electronic translators** of different types. See Chapter 23, "Useful Addresses."

CHAPTER THIRTEEN

SHOPPING

One of us had a grandmother who was a passionate world traveler. Her return from a place like Burma was always a wonderful event, partly because she always sat down with her grandchildren and had them guess what she had brought each of them. The presents were always tiny animals — a glass horse, a wooden tiger, a papier-mâché elephant — small enough to fit in one's hand. We were enchanted by the foreignness of the gifts. Not only have we treasured them ever since, but we also now believe they were the perfect type of present to bring back from a foreign place — tiny, inexpensive, and delightful.

Yet it's impossible to bring gifts to everyone to whom you'd like to. We suggest you keep to a minimum the number of people to whom you'll bring anything expensive. Inexpensive gifts could include a record; foodstuffs such as mustard, jams, chocolates, chutney; a silk scarf from Asia or a tartan scarf from Scotland; a cookbook; color slides; inexpensive handmade jewelry; or a little book of postcards.

Before you leave on your trip, find out what the **specialties of the place** are. Then check out the prices of the same items in this country. For example, can you purchase a Belleek tea service cheaper through a catalog, in an American gift shop, in an Irish or British gift shop, or at the factory shop in Northern Ireland? Travelers often complain that they think they've gotten a great deal while on a trip, only to come home and find the same item selling for less here.

Have a general idea of what you want to purchase, in order to **limit impulse buying.** Make a list, based on reading guidebooks, newspaper travel sections, and information from tourist offices.

Make another list of the people for whom you want to buy gifts, and how much you want to spend. Keep this in a little notebook to take shopping. **Know people's measurements** ahead of time, and bring along a measuring tape, since sizes will be different abroad.

Once at your destination, inquire at the tourist office about where the **best deals** may be. Are there any craft fairs? What about street markets? Are there seasonal sales, such as post-Christmas sales in January? Talk to other tourists and, even more importantly, to locals, to learn about any special shops, areas, good deals, or interesting items they've discovered.

If you have a few days to shop, spend the first one simply wandering — **window-shopping and browsing.** Bring along your notebook to record any useful information — prices, store names, differences in quality.
    On your second day, you can simply go directly to the place with the best deal — and make your purchase with confidence.

When you *do* buy something, jot down the date, the amount in foreign currency, and what you paid in U.S. dollars. Be sure to save the receipt, because you may need to show it when you come through customs. Even in this country, it's useful to **keep a record** of the date purchased and the price.

Paying by credit card means that you will be billed at the exchange rate in effect **on the day the charge clears** in the U.S., not the rate the day you made the purchase. Thus you cannot predict exactly how much you will be paying, or whether it will be more or less.

Be aware of **duty charges.** The booklet "Know Before You Go," available from the U.S. Customs Service (see Chapter 23, "Useful Addresses"), lists them for you. The duty may be so small that it's worth buying certain articles even if you will have to pay duty on them.

The $400 per person duty-free allowance applies only to the things you **carry home with you.** Anything you mail home will be subject to duty, unless it is a gift with a value of less than $50. See Chapter 16, "Coming Home."

Shipping things home is costly, but it is helpful to get your things from the shop right to your door.

Duty-free shops may not be as cheap as the United States, especially for spirits. Again, know your prices.

VAT

You must pay Value Added Tax (V.A.T. has different names in different countries), a sales tax that every resident of the country must also pay. You can get reimbursed for it (as much as 30% of the cost of an item), if you obtain a special form from the merchant. When you leave the country, you have to give the form to a customs officer, who will sign it and send it to the Customs Office. Eventually it will find its way back to your merchant, who, instead of paying that tax to the government, will send it to you.

(The rationale behind this is that although the residents of the country are taxed, the government wants to encourage *your* business. Yet if you did not have to pay the VAT at all, or if you were reimbursed on the spot, you might turn around and sell the item to a resident and make a profit for yourself.)

In order to be reimbursed, you must be certain that your shop will follow through and that you have the form signed when you leave the country. Crossing the borders of some countries involves so little formality that you could easily forget to turn the form in. If this is the case, try sending the form, signed by the U.S. Immigration Office, to the Customs Service of the country you were visiting.

BARGAINING

Bargaining has been part of buying and selling for thousands of years. You are at a slight disadvantage when bargaining with a shrewd, seasoned negotiator, because our culture does not allow us to sharpen our wits at this activity. If the seller agrees with our prices, then we think we must have started bargaining too high; yet we are reluctant to haggle too aggressively for fear of offending.

It is important to remember that there is no "right price" for items such as crafts. The right price is what both sides are comfortable with — it varies according to the context. Again, be familiar with the prices of comparable items back home.

If you are at a craft market, with many different vendors selling similar items, check what several different sellers are asking for the same object. When there's a big price discrepancy, you can ask, "Why is it more expensive here than from that man over there?" Perhaps there is a difference in quality, and the vendor will educate you. Or perhaps your question will be taken as a bargaining ploy, and the original price may come down.

Put energy into your bargaining. Merchants seem to love a **vigorous negotiation,** and may enjoy themselves enough to give you a good price.

Children are often good bargainers. They seem to have the correct combination of passion and indifference.

The best purchases are often made in the **early morning,** when the vendor is just getting up, and **at dusk,** when he or she is packing everything away. Some vendors are superstitious, and like to encourage a first sale of the day to get the morning started well. Others try to make a final sale before packing up, so that they have less to take home.

Certain goods from certain countries — usually cottage industries that don't compete with our economy, such as Mexican ceramics — are **exempted from duty.** This is called the Generalized System of Preferences. Write to U.S. Customs for a booklet called "GSP and the International Traveler" (see Chapter 23, "Useful Addresses").

BARTERING

In some parts of the world you will be able to barter. In Kenya, for example, you can barter for jewelry or for the bold printed cottons. Good things to bring along for this are T-shirts, pens, digital watches, baseball caps, socks, scarves, and sunglasses.

Be sure to shop in a **grocery store** in a foreign country. Whether it's a French supermarket or an Asian bazaar, you will enjoy the contrast of the exotic and the familiar. Bring along a net or plastic bag. In many parts of the world grocery bags do not exist, and it's customary to bring your own.

To learn about the special features of the handicrafts you buy, **go to a museum.** This might help you to distinguish quality from junk, and it will place the items in a historical and artistic context.

CHAPTER FOURTEEN

PHOTOGRAPHY

There are many reasons *not* to bring a camera along on a trip. It is cumbersome, fragile, a constant security headache — and at times being overly concerned with photographs interferes with your enjoyment. You're busy loading the camera and snapping away and you miss seeing things with your own eyes. Then if the pictures don't come out you've lost everything.

Yet you want visual records of your trip. We would like to suggest that you consider bringing an "Instamatic"-type camera — one that's inexpensive, light, small, simple to operate and not too precious to lose. It should have a built-in flash. The camera's limitations will keep you from looking at your trip through a lens. Instead you'll merely be keeping records — of friends' faces, memorable events, places, and celebrations. And if the camera is lost or stolen you won't be devastated — your biggest loss will be the roll of pictures inside it.

Or you can bring a Polaroid instant camera. Both camera and film are bulky, and are limited, but you will be able to delight your models with gifts of instant pictures. Partway through your trip, when your camera gets too heavy, you can give it to a new acquaintance.

That said, we can discuss more expensive equipment. Depending on your expertise, you may want to bring a small, fully automatic single-lens reflex camera with a built-in flash, or a simple, basic, 35-millimeter camera. If you do decide to take an expensive camera, be prepared to protect it from loss, theft, and damage throughout your trip.

If your camera is of foreign manufacture, register it with U.S. Customs before you leave this country. Otherwise you may be charged duty on it when you return. If you cannot register it, bring along the sales receipt.

Whatever camera you bring, make sure you're absolutely familiar with it before your trip. Shoot at least five rolls of film and have them developed before you go so that you can familiarize yourself with the camera and a number of different conditions — light, focus, film speed, flash, color vs. black and white film, and so on. While you're traveling you probably won't be developing film (processing film abroad tends to be much more expensive and of much poorer quality than here in the States), so you will not receive the vital feedback of seeing your photos. Know what kind of effects you can produce with your camera in different situations — action shots, portraits, landscapes. Learn how quickly you can whip it out and have it focused for that once-in-a-lifetime shot.

LENSES

When deciding what lenses to bring, ask yourself what kind of pictures you'll be taking. Wildlife and landscape photography will demand a different lens than people and action shots will.

It's convenient to have the versatility of a zoom lens, but you lose lens speed, ease of focus, and sharpness, and the lens is heavy and bulky besides. With numerous lenses, on the other hand, you lose precious minutes getting the right one on for the shot. If you solve this problem the way news photographers do, with several cameras around your neck — have you ever encumbered yourself!

Our recommendation is that you carry just one lens and that it be a fast normal lens. If you take a second lens, it could be a zoom (35 to 105 millimeter).

FILM AND BATTERIES

Make a reasonable estimate of the **amount of film** you will need for the trip. Then double it. New sights and surroundings will arouse your photographic urges. The film you buy in advance will be of excellent quality and probably cheaper than that available in most other countries.

If you have access to a slide projector at home, take color slide film. You can then have just the best shots made into prints.

In addition to the set of batteries in your camera, bring a set for **every two weeks** you'll be gone. Batteries may cost more than twice as much in a foreign country as in the United States.

When you **buy film in some less developed countries,** you have to be alert. Kodak and Ilford can cost more than ten dollars per roll. You may want to test the local brand of film, and you should try to have a roll developed to determine its quality.

Never let a shopkeeper sell you name-brand film and load it in your camera before you have made sure that the **seal is intact.** When this happened to us we found out later that the film was not in fact Kodak, but some other type, attached to a reel with a piece of adhesive tape, rolled up, and placed in a Kodak box. We were lucky that the film had not been exposed already.

Place a **haze filter** over your lens to protect it.

TAKING PICTURES

Photographers in a foreign country are like an audience in a theater. Try to photograph the local people as they play out their lives on the stage that is their home. Shoot a scene from a couple of different angles.

For us the most important photography tip is to **get up early** before dawn if possible. You can watch a place come slowly to life, and the light often has an especially evocative quality.

The other best time to take pictures, we feel, is in **late afternoon,** in what we like to call the "champagne" light.

If you will be shooting on a beach or in the desert, where the wind can whip sand into the cracks of your camera, make sure you **carry it in a case** and that you have a protective haze filter over the lens.

A common mistake travelers make is to dutifully photograph monument after monument. This can make for very boring viewing later. **Include people** in your pictures — either locals or your own group.

Make sure you **take pictures of the friends you make!** Of all your photos, these will be the ones you cherish most.

Be sure to get photos of the **local people,** in farmer's markets, at sports events, festivals, and so on.

Beware of **unusual photography situations** — snow and sand can be very bright and may throw off an automatic timing. Read your camera manual to find out how to deal with this. Bracket your exposures (take three of the same shot at different settings) if you are in a tricky situation — or taking the shot of your lifetime.

If you are taking a picture of **something enormous or something tiny,** incorporate a person or part of a person for scale.

Get close enough so that your **subject fills the frame.**

It isn't easy to photograph people discreetly. Modest women or elderly people may turn away in embarrassment or disapproval; children may overreact and pester you to take more pictures.

In some places, posing for tourists has become a real industry. Whether or not to **tip your model** has to be dealt with in context. We've never actually done this, preferring to offer to send the person a picture (and then following through!). But offering a coin may be the only way to get the exact photo you want. Beware, though, that posing for pictures may be a profitable business for your subject.

Try "shooting from the hip" — holding your camera at waist height. Practice before you go.

Every photographer mourns a **missed picture** — whether it's of a shy smile creasing a weathered face or of an elephant crossing a river at dawn. Think, though, that if that lost picture is so indelibly engraved in your memory, it's even better than if you had caught it on film.

If you **shoot from an airplane window,** try to avoid sitting where the wing will dominate your photo (although a slice of it can add some drama). Place your lens right against the window so that your picture won't pick up the scratches on the glass. The corners and edges of an airplane window are very distorted, so try to keep your camera directed out the middle.

Remember that to get good shots from a plane window you'll have to be ready **just after the plane takes off.** Within two minutes you'll be too high to make anything out.

SECURITY

Although **airport security equipment** at U.S. and European airports will not harm your film, in other countries you will have to protect it to be sure you won't lose every shot you took. Hand your film and your loaded camera to the security guard for a manual inspection.

DEVELOPING

If you decide to ship film home to your home or camera store from abroad, be sure to send it air mail. Mark the package FILM so that it will (hopefully) not be X-rayed.

In this country, you can bring along a number of **prepaid envelopes** from a mail-order film developing house. Send back the film as you shoot it, and your pictures will be waiting for you when you arrive home.

Traveler's Checklist (see Chapter 23, "Useful Addresses,") carries a handy **Film Shield** that can protect up to 22 rolls of 35-mm. film or a loaded camera from airport X-rays.

Besides X-rays, there is nothing more damaging to film than **high temperatures.** Don't leave film or your camera in the trunk of a car or in a closed, hot car.

Extreme cold can also have an adverse effect on film, making it become brittle and even crack or break. Wrap film you're about to use in something woolen, or keep a roll or two in your pockets for a short time, to keep it warm, pliable, and manageable.

CHAPTER FIFTEEN

SAFETY AND SECURITY

One of the authors was walking through an Old Delhi market one morning when a crowd of beggar women attached themselves to her, thrusting out their hands and demanding money. As she continued walking, the women became more aggressive. She turned and spoke sharply to them, and the next moment they were gone.

She felt quite proud of herself until she realized that the closed zipper on her shoulder bag had split open and her wallet was gone. And, of course, so was the band of women, vanished into one of the thousands of alleys that thread that teeming city.

Luckily, the experience served only as an inexpensive warning — the wallet contained about five dollars worth of rupees. Safely in the bag still was a camera worth $200.

Take very seriously the possibility of being ripped off on your travels, and try to manage things so that whatever you lose is not a great loss — neither important nor valuable.

Carry your true essentials — passport, tickets, traveler's checks, credit cards — on your person, preferably under your clothes in a money belt or pouch.

Leave valuable or irreplaceable items, such as jewelry, priceless documents, and furs, at home in your safety deposit box.

The rest of your belongings should then be considered replaceable, including your camera. You can bring an inexpensive camera, in order to minimize your worry. Or you can insure your camera before your trip. (See Chapter 14, "Photography.")

Once you have protected yourself in this way, you can have a relatively carefree attitude — and you won't have to end your trip if your luggage is stolen. If you are paranoid about being robbed, however, then your whole trip will be poisoned.

If you're in a country that's much poorer than the U.S., remember that your very presence betokens a degree of wealth that is inconceivable to the people you meet. If you thoughtlessly flaunt money, you could be said to deserve to be ripped off. Be discreet.

In regard to personal safety, ask the U.S. Embassy or consulate if you're in doubt about whether to enter a tense area. Follow their advice!

MONEY

Thieves often work **crowd scenes** — thronged outdoor events, crowded bus stations and airports. Some thieves specialize in robbing tourists, knowing they are carrying money. If you are going to be in a crowded place, ensure that your valuables are not visible.

The two most vulnerable places to keep your money are your **back hip pocket and a dangling handbag.** The inside breast pocket of a jacket is safer if it has a button or Velcro tab to seal it.

When you go out at night, especially in a rough neighborhood or red-light district, don't take with you more money than you can afford to lose. Leave the rest in the hotel safe or carefully hidden in your room.

If you carry a handbag or pouch, place the strap **over your head** as well as your shoulder, and then put your jacket on over the bag.

One friend recommends a **double-wallet system,** keeping only a small amount of cash in a wallet in the inside breast pocket, and keeping the rest of the money in a money belt under the clothes.

Before your trip, make sure that the zipper, clasp, and straps of your handbag or shoulder bag are **rugged and strong.** Check them periodically during your travels, and have them repaired if necessary. Remember that an overstuffed bag is likely to burst.

Wrap your wallet with **rubber bands** and it will be harder to remove from your pocket without detection.

LUGGAGE

If you are taking a long journey by train or bus, and you have to sleep, **loop your luggage straps around your arm or leg** or tie your bags to you.

In a transportation terminal, **keep your luggage with you** at all times (unless you can check it). Carry it with you even into a stall in a rest room. Do not rely on a nearby stranger to watch your bags.

Count your bags every time you get off a train or plane or out of a taxi.

Here's a tip that has been learned through hard experience. When you take a taxi, get into the habit of **noticing the driver.** If his cab carries his identification, register on his name; otherwise, notice his looks, the color and type of the vehicle, etc. We have been known to leave things in taxicabs, and have had 100 percent success in getting them back by piecing together memories of the driver and going back to the taxi stand where we caught the cab. Cab drivers may sometimes seem unethical in charging exorbitant rates, but they are likely to be honest regarding lost property.

Do not leave valuables in your car, particularly if they're visible, even if the car is locked.

Always watch as a customs official looks through your belongings. One of us had a recorder lifted by a customs official on the Peru-Bolivia border — an item that never should have been in the luggage atop the bus! Favorite things should stay right next to you.

DOCUMENTS

Before leaving on your trip, make a safety list (see Chapter 22, "Checklists"). This should include a list of traveler's check numbers, credit card numbers, airplane ticket numbers, emergency refund phone numbers, and your itinerary. Make two copies, leave one at home with a friend or house-sitter, and bring one with you in your suitcase.

Memorize your passport number and its date and city of issue. Many travelers make a photocopy of the first four pages of their passport and keep this in a safe place. It will serve as a record of the passport number and other details and will prove invaluable if you require a temporary passport in a foreign country.

Be sure to pack a half-dozen extra passport photos (ask for extra when you get the picture taken).

U.S. **passports** are worth a lot of money on the black market. Don't give yours to anyone who doesn't have a good reason to see it. Don't use it as collateral for anything. In some areas, however, you may be asked to leave your passport overnight with the hotel management. We recommend asking the desk clerk to write out a receipt for it.

If you are traveling in a country that has been the focus of attention for any of a number of reasons — natural disaster, transportation accident, change of governments, civil war, terrorism — **register your passport and itinerary** with the nearest United States embassy or consulate. You may not be in any actual danger or feel any threat, but your people back home will rest easier if there is a record of your registration.

HOTEL SAFETY

Mark the **location of your hotel** on your map, so that if you get lost and can't speak the language you can point it out to a taxi driver or police officer.

Rooms between the **third and sixth floor** of a hotel are considered safest. They are high enough to prevent entry from ground level, yet not so high that they cannot be reached by fire equipment. Next safest would be a room on the top floor for access to the roof.

If you feel your room is in an **unsafe part of the hotel** (poor lighting, far from elevator, near back stairway), ask immediately that it be changed.

When you take the room, check out where the **fire exit** is. Look on the back of the door for emergency evacuation procedures posted there by the hotel.

Don't just read emergency instructions; rehearse them. Go out into the hall and see where the exit is — count the number of doors from your room to the nearest staircase. In the event of a fire the halls can become engulfed with a smoke so thick that you have to crawl along the floor in order to breathe. You may not be able to find the stairs unless you have planned your route to get there.

Make sure that your hotel room **doors and windows lock.**

Have your room key **in your hand** before getting on the hotel elevator.

You can purchase a small **traveling security system** through Traveler's Checklist (see Chapter 23, "Useful Addresses.") This small item, about the size of a transistor radio, combines a burglar alarm, a smoke alarm, an alarm clock, and a powerful flashlight, all in one.

GENERAL SAFETY TIPS

Carry a flashlight in your pocket or purse.

Make a point of learning how to use the **local pay telephone.** Often you are not supposed to deposit coins until your party answers; if you do, you will lose your money. Save your change so that you always have the correct change with you for a phone call.

Before **swimming at an unfamiliar beach,** take the time to observe the surf. Are there other people swimming? Are they at about your level of competence? Is there a lifeguard on duty? Are there flags or other signs indicating areas that are out of bounds? Don't swim by yourself at an unfamiliar beach unless you have found a sheltered cove where the waves are gentle. We have found that even so popular a beach as Copacabana in Rio de Janeiro is not for any but the strongest swimmers. One of the authors swam there and felt lucky to emerge alive, pulled out by some young men; her friend's bathing suit was swept off. We realized afterward that no one else was swimming; it was a sunbathing beach.

If you are lucky enough to **see wildlife from your car** or tour bus, whether it's bears in Yellowstone Park or tigers in India, view them from the safety of your car. Do not get out to take a picture of a dangerous animal.

For tips on **driving safety,** see Chapter 9, "Getting Around."

IN AN EMERGENCY

It is essential to have your passport with you at all times. If you get into trouble of any kind (an accident in which you were at fault, for example), and you do not have your identification, you may be treated like a criminal.

The Overseas Citizens Emergency Center (Department of State, Washington, DC 20520, PH: 202-647-5225) will help with any complicated medical, financial, or legal problems incurred abroad. They'll notify your relatives at home, help you to receive funds, and assist with medical support.

If you are in serious medical or legal trouble overseas, contact the American consulate. They are an important resource and support while you're traveling abroad, but they will not lend you money or cash your personal check. The most they can do in this respect is to receive someone else's check or wire from the United States and hold it for you.

American Express Cardmembers can use the Global Assist service when they're in an emergency on a trip more than 100 miles from home. The toll-free hotline will refer you to a nearby legal or medical professional, will arrange for a translator if needed, and will notify your home or office. In the United States the number is 1-800-554-AMEX. Abroad, call collect 202-783-7474.

GETTING MONEY OVERSEAS

There are several ways to get funds transferred to you in a foreign country, varying in cost and efficiency.

The Cable Remittance Order is the fastest way to send money overseas. Your home bank will transfer funds to a foreign bank, which will then notify you.

The Mail Remittance Order is the same as the above, but the money is sent by air mail, not by telegram, and is thus much cheaper and slower.

Western Union has an International Funds Transfer Service, through which your friend or relative can call a toll-free number, charge up to $1,000 on their VISA or MasterCard number, and have it sent to you anywhere in the country or the world. You will be able to pick up the money at a foreign bank or post office, in local currency, one or two business days later. The person who sends the money must have the correct address.

You can also go to the telegraph office wherever you are and have them wire your bank for money.

You can write your bank and ask it to send some funds to a bank in a certain city. Have them send a message to you at your hotel or at Poste Restante saying which bank the deposit has been made in.

TELEPHONING HOME

Best phoning method is to find an international telephone and telegraph office (to be found in any major city). You give the number you wish to call to a clerk, and then wait while they dial it for you. When the connection is made the clerk calls you and gives you a private booth. You pay afterward.

LOST PASSPORT

Report the loss immediately to the American consulate or embassy. They will issue you a new passport (but you have to pay full price). If you have some passport-size pictures, a copy of your birth or naturalization certificate, and the details if your lost passport (number, date and city of issue), this process will go much more smoothly.

LOST CREDIT CARDS

Report the loss immediately to the company, using its emergency phone number. If you report the loss immediately, before the credit cards are used, you will not be liable for any unauthorized use. In any case, you are only liable for $50 for such use.

LOST TRAVELER'S CHECKS

Report the loss immediately, using the company's emergency phone number. Report the loss also to the police.

ROBBERY

Report the robbery to the police and, if it occurred in a hotel, to the management. Only if you have done so will your insurance company reimburse you.

GETTING ARRESTED

If you get arrested, get in touch with the nearest American consulate so that you have an advocate who knows the ropes.

Don't drink even a small amount of alcohol before driving. In Scandinavia having even one drink may be considered a criminal offense if you should then cause an accident.

GETTING BUMPED

If your plane is overbooked and you are in danger of being bumped, explain calmly and firmly to a supervisor that you cannot be bumped, that you have a confirmed seat, and so on. The airline personnel are required to seek volunteers before bumping people involuntarily. See Chapter 7, "Going By Plane."

LUGGAGE PROBLEMS

If your luggage is damaged or lost, act immediately. Fill out a claim form from the airline that handled the last stage of your trip. You have seven days to claim damage, twenty-one to claim loss, but especially in the case of damage, your claim will be processed more easily if you make it immediately. See Chapter 7, "Going By Plane."

AIRPLANE DELAY

If your flight is seriously delayed, ask for compensation from the airline in the form of restaurant meals or a hotel room. Airlines do not routinely dispense such amenities any more, but if you insist you may receive them. See Chapter 7, "Going By Plane."

AIRPLANE EMERGENCY

In an emergency, obey your cabin crew without question. Most important is to get out of the plane quickly to avoid a possible fire. Since most crashes occur on take-off and landing, they involve relatively low speeds.

Have your first priority be to get yourself and your children off the plane quickly. Leave everything behind. If you can leave within a minute and a half you will probably be able to avoid the fumes that will spread through the plane. If the air is filling with fumes, stay low — crawl if necessary to avoid inhaling them. Put something over your mouth and nose if there is smoke in the cabin. And get as far as possible from the plane after the crash.

Do not smoke in the rest room!

CHAPTER SIXTEEN

COMING HOME

CUSTOMS

Customs officials are checking for two kinds of things: dutiable items acquired abroad, and illicit items not allowed in this country.

Women in particular should be careful not to accept packages from recent acquaintances to deliver to "friends" in the United States. Such packages have been known to contain illegal drugs.

Take the film out of your camera. The customs official may open it.

DUTIES

Customs duties were, from 1789 to 1914, the main source of income for the U.S. government. Their purpose is to protect American products from competition with less expensive foreign goods.

Customs officials tend to be very well versed in how much things cost. If you undervalue something, and they discover this, the article will be confiscated and you will be penalized for the amount it is worth in the United States.

Have handy for customs inspection the receipts of any items you may have purchased abroad. You can order a very useful booklet, "Know Before You Go," for free from the U.S. Customs Service, Box 7407, Washington, DC 20044.

Every returning resident of the United States has a "personal exemption" of $400, meaning that $400 worth of goods acquired abroad may be brought into this country duty-free, subject to certain exemptions on liquors, cigarettes, and cigars. Items purchased abroad that fall into this category must have been acquired for your personal or household use, they must be with you and declared, and your trip must have had a duration of at least 48 hours.

Whether or not your luggage gets checked is entirely random. It's wise, therefore, if you have something to declare, to declare it.

No more than **100 cigars and 200 cigarettes** (one carton) may be included in your exemption. A duty will be imposed on anything more than this.

One liter (33.8 fluid ounces) of **alcoholic beverages** may be brought in with you duty-free if you are 21 or older and it is for your own use or a gift.

If you are returning from the **U.S. Virgin Islands, American Samoa, or Guam,** you may bring in goods, duty-free, amounting to $800. If you are 21 or older you may bring in from these islands, free of duty, five liters of alcoholic beverages (169 fl. oz.). You have to have purchased four out of five of those liters on the islands, and one out of the five must have been produced there.

If you **exceed the above exemptions,** you must pay 10% on the next $1000 worth of goods (5% if you are coming from the U.S. Virgin Islands, American Samoa, or Guam).

The following items are admitted free of duty:

Antiques produced more than 100 years ago (obtain proof of antiquity from seller)
Binoculars, opera and field glasses
Books
Diamonds, cut but not set
Drawings and paintings done entirely by hand
Exposed film (though unexposed film may be dutiable)
Natural pearls, loose or temporarily strung without clasp
Original works of art
Postage stamps

Be careful when purchasing **"works of art"** overseas. Customs officials may regard them as dutiable if they were produced by a skilled craftsman instead of a professional artist. You may pay thousands of dollars for pieces of Murano glass from Italy, for example, thinking that they are created by artists, and thus duty-free, but a customs official will say they are produced by craftsmen, and thus dutiable.

The key criteria is whether the work is original in concept, one of a kind, and produced by a professional artist. Anything mass-produced that you buy in a vendor's stall will not be considered a work of art.

With sculpture, the original is considered a work of art, as well as the first ten castings. Copies made after the first ten will be dutiable.

If you can prove that the maker of the piece is an artist you may be able to convince customs that the item should be duty-free.

If you have **purchased an automobile** overseas, it must meet U.S. safety standards and emission standards. Write the U.S. Customs Office for a leaflet called "Importing a Car."

Products from the following countries are dutiable at a much higher rate than other countries: Albania, Bulgaria, Cuba, Czechoslovakia, Estonia, East Germany, Indochina, North Korea, Kurile Islands, Latvia, Lithuania, Outer Mongolia, Poland, Southern Sakhalin, Tanna Tuva, Tibet, and the U.S.S.R.

PROHIBITED AND RESTRICTED ITEMS

Warning! Do not carry illegal drugs into or out of the United States, just because your bags have never before been searched. Customs checks are often done randomly.

Items that are prohibited by law from entering the United States are:

- most fruits and vegetables
- most meats and poultry
- absinthe
- liquor-filled candy
- lottery tickets
- live monkeys
- narcotics and dangerous drugs

■ publications and articles deemed by the official to be obscene, seditious, or treasonable

■ hazardous articles, including fireworks

■ toxic and poisonous items

■ switchblades.

Special regulations govern import of biological materials, pre-Columbian artifacts, firearms and ammunition, and South African Kruggerands.

From the U.S. Department of Agriculture, Washington, DC 20250, you can get a free booklet called "Travelers' Tips on Bringing Food, Plant and Animal Products into the United States."

MAILING THINGS HOME

If despite your best intentions you still brought too heavy a load, you can ship your personal belongings home. If you are overseas, and the items were purchased in the United States, you will not have to pay duty as long as you write on the package, "American goods returned."

You can send a **gift valued at not more than $50** to a friend duty-free, as long as the friend doesn't receive more than $50 in gift shipments in one day. Write on the outside "Unsolicited gift," what the present is, and its value. You can also send gifts to several persons in one package if they are individually wrapped and clearly marked.

Items you purchased abroad will be dutiable **if you send them to yourself.**

In Asia, where paper and tape are in short supply, you will easily find **tailors** who will stitch your articles into neat cotton bundles and seal them with wax. Make sure that the packages are clearly addressed with indelible ink, that the customs forms and stamps are firmly affixed, and that you have marked the package BY SEA (cheap but takes forever) or BY AIR.

CULTURE SHOCK

Suddenly your momentum is gone, your trip is over, and you have to resume your normal life. But your experiences have changed you. A common complaint of travelers is that no one seems interested in hearing about their extraordinary trip.

One of us has a father who loves to travel himself. Whenever we returned from a trip he'd sit down at the kitchen table and want to hear the entire story, saying "So you left here...."

We've found that the best way to depressurize after a trip is to have a party that includes a slide show or scrapbooks and a chance for you to discuss your trip. If you bought a cookbook, prepare an exotic dish or two. If you bought a native costume — a sari, a kimono, or a Hawaiian shirt, for example — this might be one of your few opportunities to wear it.

Another way to ease culture shock is to **write letters to the friends** you made on your trip. If you can, send them a photo of yourself with them, or just of yourself. We have such correspondences that date back ten years and more. When you visit the country again, you will have a place to go and a warm friendship to resume. You may also have a chance to host your friends in this country. We have found that travel gives us an entirely new understanding of the concept of hospitality.

You might also write letters to any **organizations that helped make your trip a success** — or those that did not.

HEALTH

Most illnesses acquired abroad will manifest symptoms during your trip or within two months of your return. If within a year you contract an illness, however, mention your trip to your doctor. These symptoms are particularly significant: rash; prolonged fever; persistent or bloody diarrhea; persistent and inexplicable weight loss; unexplained pain in abdomen, chest, or head.

CHAPTER SEVENTEEN

THE SOLO TRAVELER

Solo travel is a voyage into yourself. You will either thrive on the discoveries you make, or you will want to back out, quickly. People that intentionally travel alone have an instinctive sense that they'll enjoy it. You will have much more interaction with the locals. You will learn the language much more quickly (with a pair of travelers one often picks up the language faster and does the brunt of the talking). You'll be much closer to the reality of the country — and to the amazing goodness of other human beings.

But you may also have times when you wish you had a traveling companion to share a special moment or a crisis with. You can meet a companion on the road or through a service that matches travel partners (ask your travel agent about this). Many people alternate traveling alone and traveling with a partner. Before deciding to travel with someone, consult Chapter 1 to find some important questions to ask yourself.

One way to enrich a solo trip is to keep a journal. It gives you a chance to share the memorable moments and the lonely times. Many travelers later lament that they have forgotten too much about their trips. With a journal you can pin down the essence of a place — its colors, smells, sounds, the native costumes, the food you eat, the people you meet. If you're learning a language, you can jot down particularly useful words and phrases. You can record names of hotels so you'll know which to return to and which to avoid. You can collect addresses and keep track of expenses. You won't believe how precious a document this will seem five or ten years after your trip; who knows? it may even be publishable.

Common sense is the key to success for the solo traveler, says a woman we know who makes frequent business trips. The less you appear to be an "out-of-towner" in big cities, she says, the better off you'll be. She always studies a map of a city she's going to. Before giving a cab driver an address, she always has a general sense of how to get there. She gives the cabbie the street address, cross streets, and district, to let him know she knows where she's going. She sometimes keeps the map open on her lap as they drive to make sure he's not taking a round-about route. This affords a sense of security, she says, as well as sometimes reducing cab fares.

WOMEN ALONE

As a woman alone you will have unique challenges and re-wards on your trip. You have more opportunities for great travel experiences than do group travelers, couples, or single men. You will meet both women and men, both in this country and abroad, much more eas-ily than a man can. It's still unusual to see a woman traveling alone, after all, and thanks to the trust people generally feel toward women, you will have a way into the culture that men lack.

But it's a fine line for women travelers. A solo female can have a fabulous, incomparable trip, or she can have a disastrous one. You can meet people easily while traveling, but you often have to extricate your-self from people you don't like or want to be with. Some women are naturally friendly and spend a lot of time putting up with and resenting unwanted companionship; others get into the habit of coldly rebuffing all approaches and then find they feel lonely and cross.

It is certainly no more dangerous to travel than it is to stay home. In foreign countries, in particular, women seem to receive more respect than they do here. The differences are that you're somewhat more exposed (in hotel rooms and campgrounds, for example), and that you do not have a native's understanding of the culture.

Women traveling alone must do everything with a little more care and alertness than others need, including how you dress. You should do your homework ahead of time, to become familiar with exactly where you're going and how to get there, so that your ignorance is not taken advantage of. Learn as much as you can about the culture, so that you understand the status of women and the social customs of the country. For you, a smattering of the language is especially important.

Don't let your lack of knowledge become paranoia. If you're going to be paranoid, you may as well stay home.

One good rule of thumb is to follow your instincts. If a man starts talking to you in the Roman Forum, and you feel irritated or uncomfortable with him, don't let him attach himself to you for even a minute. Don't feel apologetic — you have invested a lot in this trip, and you should run things. Look him straight in the eye, without smiling or apologizing, and say (in English if you don't know the language — the message will get across) loudly, clearly and firmly that you do not wish to talk with him any more and you would like him to leave you alone. Don't worry about being rude.

If, on the other hand, you find the man attractive or trustworthy, you're in a well-populated place, and it's daytime, you may wish to accept his offer to have a coffee. Lovely romances do happen on trips. Always pay your own way so that you don't feel you owe him anything. Early on, find out his name and where he works. If he has a motorcycle or a car, notice the license number. And if you start feeling uncomfortable with him, disengage yourself firmly and immediately.

Do not drink heavily or take drugs with a man you've just met in a foreign country — especially if you don't know the language. This is a sure way to lose control of the situation.

Never let a strange man touch you, even in a brotherly way — except, obviously, for a handshake or a "helping hand." He may be testing your reaction. This is your cue to make an exit.

A trick as old as the hills can still get you out of a tight spot. **Wear a ring** on your ring finger. If you wear a decorative ring, slip it around so it looks like a wedding band. Should you find yourself the object of someone's desires just excuse yourself firmly by declaring your marital fidelity and flashing the wedding band to prove it.

In Third World countries, you may find that women are warm and interested in you, your trip, and your life back in America — particularly your marital status and how many children you have. Conversation with native women in some countries may revolve around these subjects, or possibly cooking or crafts. Other times you will meet women who are highly educated, extremely articulate, and self-possessed, who will challenge you with questions about your own country.

In some countries you will be so unusual that you will be treated like a "third sex." In Venezuela, for example, one of many countries where the women serve the men and then disappear into the kitchen to eat their own meals, you would undoubtedly be served with the men (and watched through the door).

IN THE HOTEL

This may be obvious, but it is worth repeating. Convey a friendly but strong impression to the hotel staff. Do not flirt or be excessively familiar with male staff. This may be perceived as an invitation — to the very people who know your room number and have a master key. We have experienced every nuisance from banging on our hotel room door to a stealthy trying of the knob. If this happens to you, take immediate action. Call the front desk and report this if you have a telephone in your room. If you don't have a phone, go to the door and roar, "Go away or I'll call the police!" An aggressive response on your part is generally not part of your visitor's expectations.

Discourage desk clerks from **"announcing" your room number** out loud when you're checking in. It's quite easy for a "lonely man" standing behind you in line to decide to call you or drop by your room.

When you are shown to your room, **examine it before you tip the bellboy.** Make sure lights work, doors and windows lock, and the television operates.

Sometimes **single rooms are less attractive** than doubles, and women in particular may feel they are given less desirable rooms. If the price is right, you may not mind. If you feel it's unsatisfactory — isolated, for example, or having a view directly at a blank side of a building — go back to the desk clerk and ask for a different room. Make your request upon first seeing your room, not after moving in.

Have **your key in your hand** before leaving the hotel lobby to go to your room. Then you won't be fumbling in your handbag for it in an unlighted hallway.

Notice **who gets on the elevator** with you. Don't get on the elevator alone with a person whose looks you don't like. If you sense you are being followed in a hotel corridor, one trick some women recommend is to bang on their own door (or even a stranger's door if necessary) and shout a man's name. Be cautious and alert, but not overly paranoid.

Don't **go swimming late at night** by yourself in the hotel pool. You'll be especially vulnerable there.

A woman alone might reject a room that's located **right next to a back stairway,** or on the ground floor. Any of these situations, being easily accessible, are potentially dangerous. You may wish to request a room closer to the elevator (although this can be noisy in an old hotel).

DINING

Many women would love to travel solo except for the lonely prospect of sitting by themselves in restaurants day after day. One thing to remember is that being alone can be a very positive experience, even at a restaurant table. It can be an opportunity to observe people, to strike up a conversation with people at a neighboring table, to get a knowledgeable waiter's food and wine recommendations, or simply to be able to concentrate totally on a delicious meal. A lone man doesn't appear lonely and miserable; a lone woman shouldn't feel she gives that impression either.

An alternative to eating alone is to eat a meal **in your room,** if you bring along an immersible water heater, packets of tea or instant coffee, and fresh fruit or rolls.

Room service in a nice hotel can be convenient and elegant, but it is expensive. Try it once.

If you feel you've been given an **inferior table** (by the kitchen, for example), the place is not obviously crowded, and this is important to you, politely but firmly ask for a better table. Ask to speak to the manager if necessary, and be prepared to go somewhere else. You are just as important and deserve as good treatment as any other patron.

The best solution we've found to this problem is this: when you make your reservation or, if none are required, when you enter the restaurant, **inform the maitre d'** that you are a single woman and would like a good, private table. Ask if there will be any problem.

Don't, however, expect things to be the way they are at home. Service may move at a slower pace than you're used to, especially in tropical countries — Central America, the Caribbean, Africa, India — and you may not have adjusted. It helps to be patient — we've known a woman who stormed out of three Indian restaurants in one hour and never realized the problem lay with her. She was simply too prickly and impatient.

Other solutions to the problem of eating alone:

■ Bring a novel, your guidebook, or some background reading to peruse or some postcards to write while you await your order.

■ Sit at a table along the wall to feel less self-conscious.

■ Sit with another single person — and don't be surprised or offended if another single joins you, especially in Europe.

■ If you belong to an organization, see if it has chapters (meetings, clubs, etc.) in a city you'll be visiting. Some clubs have chapters all over the world that meet regularly. Try to arrive early so that you can introduce yourself to one of the members. Before the meeting's over you'll have a host of new friends.

■ Getting out and walking at noon or purchasing take-out food and eating in a park with office workers can be more fun than eating lunch in a restaurant.

■ Make a tour of some good local restaurants and enjoy your meal!

PERSONAL SAFETY

Your appearance is especially important when traveling alone. Be aware of cultural norms. Although shorts and hiking boots may be acceptable vacation gear in Sweden, they would shock people in Pakistan, where women are in "purdah" and men normally cannot even see their eyes. In many countries, women are expected to dress modestly. And in some places, the rules are not as explicit, but women dressed in jeans and T-shirts find themselves being harassed. Dressing with dignity is essential.

Unfortunately, even in a crowd you may find yourself in a difficult or annoying situation. Sometimes you have to evaluate whether to leave or make a scene.

If you are the only woman in a crowd when one or more men start bothering you, you must be especially firm and prompt in stopping the harassment. In some cases, other men may come to your rescue, but don't count on it. Stay calm, look the obnoxious fellow in the eye, speak in a strong voice, and do not let the slightest self-doubt creep into your mind.

An experience that befalls many female travelers in Europe is that in a very tight crowd a man will press against them in a most objectionable way. The only thing to do is to turn and push the man away from you, hard. This behavior toward girls and women of all ages should be objected to strenuously.

In India there is a phenomenon called "Eve-teasing," a euphemism for when a man touches a woman improperly, usually on a bus or in a crowd. This is illegal in India, and if such an incident is reported to the bus driver he is supposed to drive the bus directly to a police station. If this does happen to you (as it does to Western women, especially those who wear Indian dress), do not ignore it. If possible, grab the offender and accost him angrily. However, try not to confuse the normal crush of life in a crowded country with assaults on your honor — India is a very intimate place, and you will frequently be in close physical contact with other people.

If you are driving alone in a city, **keep your car doors locked** at all times and your windows rolled up high enough so that no one can reach in.

Good places to rest while walking through a city are **churches or hotel lobbies.**

Sometimes your **sense of humor** has to come to the rescue. One of us once wanted to climb the stairs to the top of a minaret to see the view of the old city surrounding a certain mosque. To her surprise and disappointment, she discovered that unescorted women could not go up in the minaret. When a bent, white-bearded, 88-year-old man gallantly offered to be her escort, she had to laugh. She realized she would not change centuries of Moslem tradition in five minutes, and asked a male tourist from Scotland if he would accompany her.

Club Med is often described as a good place for single women. It isn't cheap, but you get a great deal for the money — meals, sports instruction, entertainment, and a great location. At meals you sit at a table for eight, so you never have to eat by yourself.

And single-parent families find Club Med very attractive. Children are encouraged at most of the resorts. Under the age of eight they are free; from age eight to eleven, they are half-price.

The ambience of the different "vacation villages" varies, however. Find out ahead of time if your degree of sophistication matches the resort's by talking to your travel agent and to people that have been there.

CHAPTER EIGHTEEN

TRAVELING WITH CHILDREN

Traveling successfully with children depends on accepting the fact that your trip will be very different than if you were on your own. You probably won't be pub crawling or dancing until dawn (although you can find excellent babysitters if you do); instead you'll be up early watching the barges along the Seine or enjoying the marionette show at the Tivoli Gardens.

Before the trip, it's essential to involve your child in the plans and anticipation. Let her know where you're going, show her some colorful brochures, and describe some of the things you'll be doing. "We'll be flying on an airplane," you might say, "until we get to St. Louis. Then in St. Louis we'll go to a zoo, and we'll go up in a big silver arch, and we'll see the Mississippi River." Imagine what your child would most like to do — go to an amusement park? A zoo where he can pat animals? Or out in a canoe? Of course, if you promise your child you'll be doing something he's excited about, it goes without saying that you should remember to do it.

In planning your trip, think about your family's habits — your favorite activities, both separately and as a group, how you solve problems and make decisions. How well do your children get along together? Do they need constant adult supervision? Can they get absorbed in activities for a long time or do they need to move on to something new? How do they behave in restaurants? What do they most like to do — active play? Making things? Being read to? With these answers you can plan your trip to accommodate the personalities involved.

One book we can't recommend highly enough is *Fielding's Europe with Children*, by Leila Hadley (New York: William Morrow, 1984). This book would be a delight for even a non-parent to own, for it lists in detail the most "sheer fun" attractions to be found in 20 European countries from Finland to Portugal, Ireland to Greece. It includes information on flying with kids, health, water and food, diapering in a foreign land, babysitters, camps, castles, camping, and pen pals.

A typically good Hadley idea is the homecoming party, to which family, close friends, even the children's teacher and librarian are invited. Activities would include eating the food of the area, which the author suggests you send home by mail (Swiss chocolates, Scottish shortbread), listening to the music, displaying and giving away the odds and ends you picked up (a beautiful shell from a Greek beach, a postcard of Paris) and, most important, viewing your slides or scrapbooks of the trip. (For more on a slide show party, see Chapter 16, "Coming Home.")

We also recommend a marvelous service called **Travel With Your Children** (see Chapter 23, "Useful Addresses"), which will send you, for a fee, a newsletter (*Family Travel Times*) and specific information sheets.

Children can be great company on trips to places more exotic than this country and Europe. We know children who have traveled with their parents through India, trekked in Nepal, and viewed game in Kenya. Children speak a universal language, and you will find that they bring out the very best in people. You'll see smiles shining out from otherwise impassive faces; women in particular will often relate to the kids where they'd be too shy to talk to you alone. In most every situation in the Third World there are kids around or involved, so you won't feel that yours are especially loud or annoying. And reliable babysitting help is available at a very reasonable rate — check with the U.S. Consulate.

Junior high school age seems the very best time for kids to travel with their parents. They are old enough to understand and remember what they see, yet they are not so grown up that they are constantly wanting to escape from the family. At this age travel to an exotic place can be a profound, incomparable education — one of us still remembers the amazement with which she experienced the bazaar in Old Jerusalem at the age of twelve.

When you're making your plans, you can alternate a "child's day" with an "adult's day," or an afternoon with a morning — integrating zoos with art museums, amusement parts with wineries. Or you can divide up for the afternoon — your partner can take the kids to a beach while you go shopping.

The most important guideline is to slow your pace to that of your kids, not to rush them around. Plan for resting time, for ice cream eating time. Expect things to take a little longer than usual. Not only will the kids be happier if they are not rushed, but you will have some very special travel experiences, the world seen through their eyes. Don't let yourself be easily embarrassed by your kids in a strange place — try to understand their feelings, and be on their side.

As one mother puts it, all places are for kids, if you make them accessible and understandable. Try taking them to an art museum. Your attention may be entirely on your kids — and that can be fine if they are enjoying themselves. Show them why you like a particular painting — give them a way in to it. There might be a certain theme they could look for (ships, horses, etc. — who can spot them?). Talk to them in advance about what they'll see. Tell them about the artist's life.

If there's one thing in a **museum** you particularly want to see, go there first. Otherwise your kids' enthusiasm may wane before you get there.

Encourage your child to **keep a diary,** with thoughts and feelings about the trip as well as sketches of what they see.

As with all budget travelers, **lunch can be your big meal.** Restaurants seem more tolerant of energetic kids at lunchtime than at dinner. The same dish can be much cheaper. And your kids may be in a better mood.

Picnics are always fun, indoors and out. Whether it's a rest area, a beach, a park bench, or a nice meadow by a stream, you can relax, roughhouse, kick off your shoes and socks, and so on. You can also picnic at night in your motel room, after having your main meal at lunch. (For more on picnics, see Chapter 9, "Getting Around" and Chapter 11, "Dining.")

Bed and breakfast places are ideal for families traveling with kids. The atmosphere is usually much more relaxed than in a hotel or motel. Children will particularly enjoy staying on a working farm. When you call or write for reservations, mention the number of kids you're bringing and their ages.

In a foreign country, you and the children can **learn the language together.** While you're still at home, buy a foreign language instructional tape and listen to it with the kids. For your trip, purchase a phrasebook. You can quiz each other while waiting for a meal or a train. Good words to start everybody with: please, thank you, excuse me, and the numbers.

Remember that in many foreign countries children are expected to behave in a **more restrained manner** than they do in the United States and, in particular, to show courtesy toward elderly people.

If you're traveling to a country whose sanitation may be poor, bring **powdered milk** to mix with boiled water for your toddler, rather than depending on local milk. (See also Chapter 4, "Health.")

Never pass up a chance for the kids to use a bathroom. The most reliable places to find **rest rooms** while traveling are train and bus stations and hotels. Restaurants and coffee shops will usually have them in the back, and if your child needs to use the toilet, don't be embarrassed if you're not ordering anything to eat. In an emergency, shopkeepers may offer their facilities.

Throughout much of the world, the word "toilet" or "WC" will be understood.

WHAT TO TAKE

Each child should have a **small knapsack** for personal possessions — a new book or two, crayons and paper, stickers, Play-Doh, a diary, or other toys. In the outside pocket, slip a little flashlight and a little memo pad and pen. This knapsack will be the child's own property, where he can stick any special treasures accumulated on the trip. He should help choose the toys and pack them. If he's big enough (age two is big enough) he should carry it himself.

One mother we know takes her daughter shopping a few days before the trip to purchase new crayons and other items for her pack — which she then has to **save for her trip.** This makes the girl always anxious to get going on the trip so that she can open her pack and use her new toys.

Puzzles are only fun until a piece gets lost. If you do bring one, make sure it's small enough to fit on an airplane or train tray table. Count the pieces when you take them out of the box and again when you put them back in.

In addition to bringing a flashlight for each child, bring your own **nightlight** (with an adaptor if you're abroad). If your baby or children awaken at night and are scared in an unfamiliar room, it may reassure them to be able to see. Also, one parent can move around and take care of problems without awakening everyone in the room.

For the first meals away, you may wish to bring food that is **familiar to your toddler** — breakfast cereal, for example, or her favorite kind of noodles. If the child is a fussy eater, there is no reason to believe he or she will eat better with foreign foods.

Be sure to bring a box of **foil-wrapped moist towelettes.** Take them out of the box and put some everywhere you might need them — in your purse, your glove compartment, your diaper bag, your carry-on bag, your kids' knapsacks, the outside pockets of your suitcases.

Drinking straws are handy for children to use for bottled drinks especially in less developed countries.

Bring a roll of **plastic bags** (removed from the box). You'll use them for soiled diapers, wet bathing suits, shoes, laundry, and a million other things.

Airplanes are invariably **chilly,** so be sure everyone has a sweater. Trains are usually cool, as well (though occasionally you find yourself in a car that's roasting). If you're going to be on a train into the night you might want to bring blankets or sleeping bags to curl up in.

As with adults, children should bring their **favorite clothes,** things they enjoy wearing. You don't want to drag around something the child refuses to put on. Clothes that don't wrinkle or show dirt easily are important. In a hot climate, the fabric should include a fair percentage of cotton.

One mother we know buys her two children a few outfits at the local department store just before a trip — coordinating wash-and-wear shorts and tops in bright colors.

If you pack children's clothes **on child-sized hangers,** unpacking and packing will be faster. *(See also Packing Checklist, Chapter 22.)*

EN ROUTE BY CAR

If you've got a long way to go and you're driving with kids, **get an early start** — perhaps even before they're awake — and let them sleep a few hours while you drive. Have juice, a thermos of coffee, and some donuts or granola bars available for when they wake up. Then stop somewhere for breakfast.

Be sure to **stop driving every hour and a half** or two to give everyone a chance to run around, toss a football, use the bathroom, or get a drink or a snack.

Anticipate tiredness and hunger. Don't get into the position of driving around looking for a restaurant when the kids are faint with hunger, or a motel when they're exhausted.

If you stop driving for the day in the **early afternoon,** you will have plenty of time to do something fun and find your place to stay.

Share the **details of the budget** with the kids. Let them know there is a certain amount of money to be spent every day. If they can see that there is money set aside for something like a horseback ride, it might help minimize the pleas for trinkets or coins for video games.

A road atlas is not only essential but also fun, since in addition to the bound maps they have information on history, geography, landmarks, and agriculture or industry, which you can read aloud during an otherwise tedious drive.

A child that can read fairly well might enjoy having his or her own **road map and compass.** Spend a few minutes showing your child how to use the map — the key, the index, and so on.

One family we know allots **different travel tasks** to the different children. One keeps track of the budget — how much is spent each day compared to how much was planned — and writes expenses down in a logbook. Another keeps track of the route — charting it with a colored pencil on the road map. These tasks can be fun, they are great practice for the kids, and, of course they are a big contribution.

"Car packs," one imaginative mother tells us, are worth a million dollars. You can custom-make them to fit your car seats.

Stuff the pack with all sorts of useful paraphernalia: pens, pencils, pads, pocket games, coloring books, tracing paper, dot-to-dot books, and all sorts of compact (one-piece if possible) toys.

These parents wait until the night before a long trip to "stuff" the packs, one for each child. They distribute new toys for the trip among the old favorites. Then they add a couple of dollars for each child as spending money on the trip. It's always fun, these parents tell us, when the children open their carpacks at the beginning of a trip — just like opening a Christmas stocking.

CAR PACK

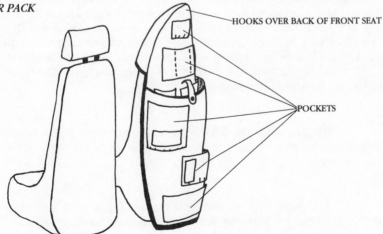

HOOKS OVER BACK OF FRONT SEAT

POCKETS

Writing on one's lap in a car is difficult. **"Lap desk" pillows,** sold in gift shops, are ideal for the car. These are pillows that mold comfortably to the lap and are topped by a hard plastic writing surface. They can later be used at home when the child is sick in bed!

It's also helpful if each child has his own little **shoebox full of car treats** to eat — apples, dried fruits, fresh vegetable sticks, candies to suck on, and so on. They can ration their own treats and not always be clamoring to stop for snacks. Place in each box a couple of packets of small moist towelettes for wiping up sticky hands.

Be sure to toss in a **roll of paper towels.**

Some **favorite car toys:** "Popomatic Bingo;" "Magic Slates;" "Pocket-Pal" games; magnetic tic-tac-toe and, for older children, chess; "Etch-a-Sketch;" quiz books with magic pens that illuminate the correct answer; funny fill-in-the-blank books; pocket quiz games; punch-out paper dolls.

Toys we recommend you **don't take** in the car: games with little pieces, which fall and get lost; crayons, which can melt in a hot car and smell terrible in the enclosed space. Pack colored pencils (with a little portable pencil sharpener) or washable colored pens instead.

If you have a **cassette player,** tape yourself reading the children's favorite stories. Then bring along both the books and the tapes, so that the kids can listen to the story and follow along with the book. This will save mom and dad from getting queasy trying to read aloud. Bring extra batteries. Packaged book and tape combinations are more expensive but the better ones have good orchestration and funny noises. A toddler will be spellbound for an hour listening to a tape of Maurice Sendak or Beatrix Potter stories.

Singing while you drive is fun and funny, especially if you have a songbook for easily forgotten words. Bring some blank tapes so that you can make your own tapes while driving.

For older children, **personal Walkman-type stereos** are the best way to go. They can listen to their own music, not to their parents' music or their little sister's story tape. They can tune out, go to sleep more easily when they want to, and so on. Be sure they have extra batteries.

Whether you're on a train or in a car, it is helpful to **tell stories** about what you're seeing. "There's a big truck from Florida and it's got oranges inside!" you might say. Or, "I see a lighthouse! Who do you think lives there?"

Have a supply of **brochures** along to show the kids where they are and where they're going. Bring a cardboard file case to keep these in.

Trucks are eternally interesting. Take a book about trucks out of the library before your trip. Your child will enjoy learning the different types of trucks, the "anatomy" of an 18-wheeler, the different phases of the journey, and what the driver's life is like. If you're at a truck stop, say hello to a driver. Your child may get a chance to see the sleeper, the gearbox, and the CB radio.

At an auto-parts store you can get a **plastic armrest** with a storage compartment inside. One or two of these would be handy for placing between siblings in the back seat, as a natural divider and a place to keep maps, books, drawing and writing materials, a travel log, and/or snacks.

EN ROUTE BY AIR

Make your reservations early. If you can fly at off-peak hours, your trip will be easier all around — shorter lines, more room on the aircraft — and you'll have the best chance of getting a free seat for your infant or toddler.
On most airlines, children up to age two can travel free if they don't need a seat. They are not, however, guaranteed seats, although airline personnel make an effort to keep an empty seat next to a parent with a "lap baby."

If it is tempting to tell the airline that a child is two, when he or she is actually older, in order so that they can travel free, remember that if the plane is full you'll be sitting with that child on your lap throughout the entire flight. One trip across the Atlantic with a 25-

pound child in your lap, plus all the paraphernalia, with only one meal to share between you, may convince you to **pay for the child's seat** next time.

Ask your travel agent or reservations clerk for **early seat selection.** Although the airline may automatically give you a bulkhead seat, we find that regular aisle seats are more convenient when traveling with an infant. There is more luggage stowing space, there are fold-down tables (not always present in bulkhead seating), you can get up when you need to, and you can stretch out your feet in the aisle. The advantage to bulkhead seats is that you can have your own little world there, especially good for toddlers, who can color or play with puzzles at your feet and can even stretch out and nap there.

On a night flight, **take your child in pajamas,** and then change her into day clothes before you land. On overnight flights, take the child's nightwear and change her into it once you're on board. Any familiar "going-to-bed" rituals, such as a stuffed animal or bedtime story, will help induce sleep.

Remind your child not to **kick the seat** in front of him. This is extremely annoying to the person sitting there.

If you're traveling with an infant, a **lightweight collapsible "umbrella" stroller"** is handy for the airport all the way up through the jetway or across the tarmac to the door of the aircraft. At that point, it can be stored in the front of the plane (for no extra charge). Just don't forget it when you disembark!

If you wish your baby to use a **"skycot"** — an airplane bassinet — be sure to reserve it in advance. All airlines have a few of these available for babies. Otherwise you can bring your baby's carry-cot free of charge, with diapers, blankets, a change of baby clothes, and a supply of baby food.

A week or so before the trip, take **a book about planes** out of the library and read it to your child.

It is easiest if you **bring your own baby food** with you. If you order 24 hours in advance, however, the airline will provide a baby meal of strained meat and vegetables, but you will need your own supply of milk, juice, crackers, fruit, cheese, or yogurt. Bring food in little jars or plastic containers that you can throw away after you've used them.

The flight attendant will **warm a baby bottle** for you. Try to anticipate when your baby will need it, so he isn't crying for it when the rest of the passengers are being served.

Make sure your carry-on luggage contains everything not only for the plane but also for the **first 24 hours of your trip.** If you're traveling with a baby, include disposable diapers (the airplane may have a small supply, but don't count on it), a bib, plenty of baby juices, disposable towels, a change of clothes for the baby, and a cloth diaper to lie her on while she's being changed.

Most airplanes do not provide a good place to **change a baby** (although this is slowly changing). Ask the flight attendant if there is a block of empty seats where you can change him — otherwise you'll have to use your seat.

During take-off, **hold your infant or toddler on your lap** (not inside your seat belt) even if there's an empty seat next to you.

As the plane takes off and lands, the **change in cabin pressure** affects the eustachian tubes in the ears. Adults and older children must yawn vigorously, chew gum or close mouth, hold nose, and try to softly blow. Your baby, however, may suffer earaches. The best solution is to let the baby nurse or drink from a bottle or a cup during take-off and landing (this might even put him to sleep!).

Have in your diaper bag **enough juice to last the journey** and the first part of your trip. The cabin air will be very dry and babies especially can become dehydrated.

EN ROUTE BY TRAIN

Trains are the ideal way to travel with children. There's plenty to do and see both out the window and on the train. Where planes quickly become nothing more than a confined space with nothing to see out the window, trains have the best scenery and lots of room to walk around.

Look at your route on a map ahead of time, so that you know what towns and landmarks you'll be passing. This can guide you in choosing which side of the train to sit on — if you're going by train from New York City to Montreal, for example, you might want to sit so that the kids can look out at the Hudson River.

When traveling with kids, the best places to sit are: near other kids; near the bathroom; near the snack bar. Try to find a seat that has all of these advantages!

As with any form of travel, be sure to have a **supply of toys** for your child.

If you let your child sit in the **window seat,** and you take the aisle seat, her attention will be directed more toward the world passing outside than to the other passengers, and you can monitor her comings and goings. You might wish to remember that if you're worried that other passengers will be bothered.

Trains and train stations are grimier than planes and airports. Have the kids dress in **jeans and overalls** rather in the "Sunday best" children used to wear "visiting." If you want them to look fresh and neat upon arrival, they can change into clean clothes in the rest room about half an hour before you reach your destination.

Even when traveling by train, where your suitcases are normally within reach above your seat, it makes sense to have a **carry-on bag.** This can hold snacks, juice, diaper changing supplies, a change of clothes for your child, and possibly an extra toy to surprise him when he has played with all of those he packed himself in his knapsack.

If you have room in your luggage, take a **picnic basket** or a child's lunchbox packed with sandwiches, fruit, crackers, and other things to nibble on. Your child can purchase drinks at the snack bar. Food is expensive on a train.

Your baby can travel in a **carry-cot,** which will allow her to watch the world flashing by or drift off to sleep — you won't even have to awaken her upon arrival at your destination. This is much easier and more comfortable than having her sleep on your lap or on the seat itself.

UNACCOMPANIED MINORS

Children between the ages of eight and eleven can travel alone on Amtrak if their trip will be completed in the daytime and if there will be no changes of train. They must, however, receive approval from the general manager of the station of origin. Children twelve and up can travel overnight.

On airplanes, children between five and eleven can travel alone, but the airlines prefer that the flight be direct, with no connections. The person meeting the child must have identification, and, in some cases, a prearranged code word. A child escort service can be arranged to assist the child through customs, passport, and security.

CHAPTER NINETEEN

THE OLDER OR DISABLED TRAVELER

Travel no longer belongs only to the young and able-bodied. In fact, travelers that are elderly or disabled often have especially wonderful trips, simply because they have to have an extra helping of the very qualities that make travel successful — resourcefulness, adventurousness, cheerfulness, a sense of humor, and careful planning.

THE OLDER TRAVELER

Senior citizens and retirees have become a major part of the traveling public, and the travel industry is courting them with a wide array of discounts and special deals. As always, however, you must ask for your discount or you may not receive it. To facilitate things, carry identification with proof of your age and membership in senior organizations.

Foreign travel is an excellent bet for the older person. In most other countries of the world, you will find, older people are far more honored than they are in the U.S.A.

If you're over 50, you can join the **American Association of Retired Persons** (AARP). This organization has a travel service (see "Useful Addresses") that designs tours, cruises, and holiday packages especially for senior travelers. In addition, their card will allow you to receive discounts on some airlines, many hotels, rental cars, and more.

Membership in the AARP is only $5 a year, so there's no reason not to join!

If you're a retiree you may have a flexible schedule that permits you to travel at **off-peak hours**. This way you can avoid the stress of long lines and you may also save money. Try to fly mid-week, midday, or Saturday. Avoid traveling on Mondays and Fridays, which are heavy travel days.

Thirty days before departure date, call the airline for an **advance seat assignment**. The most comfortable and accessible seats are on the aisle and toward the front of the aircraft. The bulkhead seats have extra leg-room. Remember, however, that you may be sitting next to parents with babies.

Seniors, especially, need to travel light. You want to be sure that you can **carry all your belongings yourself** when you need to. For walking through the airport, portable wheels on your suitcase are handy — but make sure that they won't be cumbersome for the many times you will have to carry them (getting into buses and cabs, climbing stairs, getting over curbs).

Plan to arrive at the airport in **plenty of time** — at least an hour ahead of departure time for domestic flights, and two hours for overseas flights. Watch the television monitors for information on departure times and gate assignments.

Most airlines offer **early boarding** to elderly passengers needing assistance.

Wear **comfortable clothing** for the flight. Bring along some slipper socks to wear during the flight, and an eyeshade or ear plugs if the muted din of an airplane will disturb you.

One of us had a grandmother who traveled the world with a packet of good tea and a bone china teacup wrapped up in her lingerie. Think of ways you can **pamper yourself** while you're on your trip. Perhaps it's a down pillow — you can buy one that will squash down to nothing in your suitcase. You'll find that being able to indulge in a familiar custom in a strange surrounding will give you a sense of security, even luxury.

A wonderful organization that caters only to older travelers is **Elderhostel.** You can study at universities and colleges all over the world. See Chapter 23, "Useful Addresses."

Medicare does not pay for expenses incurred abroad. You may, however, have adequate health and travel insurance through Blue Cross/Blue Shield policies, your homeowner's policy, or some of the special travel insurance policies offered by some credit card companies. If you think you do, **check the benefit details** carefully, because some policies have geographic exclusions.

If you are over 70, you may not be eligible for travel insurance in your usual plan. If you want supplemental coverage for a trip outside the U.S., contact AARP Insurance at (800) 523-5800, or, in Pennsylvania, (800) 492-2024.

One experienced traveler we know recommends that you run through in your mind all the potential snafus of your trip. Then visualize how you will cope with them. In many cases, **proper planning** can alleviate your anxieties. For example, if you are concerned about missing a plane connection, schedule extra time between flights — two hours may be better than one. If you are concerned about getting around with your baggage, either pack very light or bring along a set of collapsible wheels that can be folded up when not needed. If you are concerned about health emergencies, join an "assistance" plan (see Chapter 4, "Health"). Think through all such potential problems and anticipate their solutions.

Many discounts exist if you **ask for them** and have proof of your age. For example, seniors and disabled travelers receive 25 percent off all regular one-way Amtrak fares of $40 or more, except on Metroliners.

THE DISABLED TRAVELER

The sheer numbers of wheelchair travelers have prompted the travel industry to compete for the disabled market. There is a wealth of guidebooks and services available, airports and hotels become more accessible every day, and dozens of travel agencies now specialize in vacations for the disabled traveler. So much is possible — we have friends who have traveled in wheelchairs through South America, Africa, and India, as well as Europe and North America.

In Chapter 23, "Useful Addresses," you will find the names of some excellent books and services. In particular, you might subscribe to a travel newsletter called "The Itinerary," published by Robert Zywicki, president of Whole Person Tours, which operates tours in Europe and the U.S. for the disabled traveler. The address is P.O. Box 1084, Bayonne, NJ 07002 (201-858-3400).

If, however, you would like to make your own arrangements, or if you're headed somewhere exotic that isn't covered in a guidebook, here are a few tips to keep in mind while planning.

■ Have your wheelchair checked by a wheelchair mechanic before you go. Bring along a tool kit and spare axle.

■ Travel at less busy times — midweek, midday, Saturday.

■ Tell the reservation clerk of your disability.

■ Take a nonstop or direct flight so that you need not change planes.

■ Arrive at the airport early. You will "preboard" the plane.

■ Put a baggage tag on your wheelchair, which will probably be transported in the baggage compartment. Make sure it will be brought to the door of the plane when you reach your destination, and not to the baggage claim.

■ Crutches and canes may be stowed under your seat if they do not stick out into the aisle.

■ Guide and hearing dogs can travel on board a plane with their owners, free of charge. They are supposed to sit or lie at your feet. If you are going to a foreign country, however, there may be a quarantine that applies to your dog.

Questions to ask when making an airplane reservation:

Does the airline have any special requirements? For example, will they require that you be accompanied? Sometimes the airline will waive such a requirement if you seem competent and confident.

What type of aircraft is it — wide-bodied or narrow-bodied?

Where will your wheelchair be stowed?

Does the particular flight have jetways for boarding and disembarking? If not, how will you get on and off the plane? Some airlines have a narrow boarding chair; others use a lift.

Are special seats assigned to wheelchair passengers?

If you cannot walk, you will require assistance in order to use the rest room. However, in the future it is likely that airplanes and airplane rest rooms will be designed to accommodate wheelchairs.

The pilot should **radio ahead** if you'll need assistance, and an escort will help you pass through customs and immigration.

Many hotel chains now have a policy of accessibility. It makes sense to patronize those companies that have made this effort. The chains include Holiday Inn, Hyatt, Sheraton, Hilton, Marriott, Howard Johnson, and Quality Inns.

In this country, both Greyhound and Trailways have special plans that allow one disabled person and one companion to travel for the price of one.

Write for a free copy of *Access Travel: A Guide to Accessibility of Airport Terminals,* from the Consumer Information Center, Pueblo, CO 81009.

CHAPTER TWENTY

TIME-SHARING AND HOME EXCHANGE

What's a person to do if he or she: 1) can't afford a vacation home, 2) doesn't want the responsibility of maintaining a second home, 3) needs to carefully budget vacation expenses, 4) doesn't want the hassle of making vacation arrangements? Any or all of the situations above can be solved with the purchase of a time-share or shared-ownership property. This young industry has sought, found, and satisfied a sizable market of American vacationers. In the United States alone there are more than 1,000 time-share resorts with one-week prices that range from $2,000 to $20,000.

The idea of shared ownership started at a Hawaiian vacation development in 1969, and has gained in popularity ever since. A time-share vacation appeals to people and families from all parts of the world and the economic spectrum, but it's a commitment that may not be right for everyone. Approach it in the same way that you would any other major expense.

The beauty of a time-share vacation is that, to a great extent, it stabilizes your vacation expenses for as long as you own your time-share property. You purchase a period of time (usually measured in weeks) at a resort. There are two kinds of purchase arrangements (discussed below) that entitle you to a property at a particular time of the year, either indefinitely or for a fixed number of years. Some time-share contracts specify exactly which cottage, condominium, room or apartment you will have, while others allow you to stay in any number of similar accommodations in your price range. Some lock you into a specific week or weeks, but others only ask that you vacation during the season in which you purchased time. These are things to inquire about when you get down to signing a contract.

169

Prices can vary by thousands of dollars depending on the resort you choose, the particular unit you want to occupy, and the time of the year you vacation there. You can expect to pay more for a time-share in a warm climate during the winter, or for a ski lodge when the snow is flying. But as with hotels and other vacation suppliers, there are "high" (prime), "medium," and "low" seasons in the time-share industry. With a little flexibility you could save a bundle by taking your vacation at one or the other end of a high season at a popular resort. For instance, head in the sunny climes in October or April rather than January, and you could not only save money, but even avoid some of the hassles and headaches of contending with lots of other vacationers all demanding attention during the peak season.

It sounds glamorous, but if you are considering paying $8,000 or $10,000 for a time-share vacation (just about average for a high season week at an attractive resort) you need to look long and hard at the place and yourself. A salesperson will give you all kinds of reasons to buy a time-share property, but only you know for sure what is best for you. Ask yourself these questions:

■ Do you love this place enough to come back for 10 or 15 years or even longer? This question may seem ridiculous in the first blush of enthusiasm for a resort, but *really* try to imagine how you and your family will feel down the road. Does the resort have the facilities to keep you and your family happy for many vacations to come — and most especially, as your children become teenagers and young adults?

■ Is the resort accessible? If it costs you aggravation and lots of money to get everyone to the resort, is it going to be worth the effort to repeat the pilgrimage every year? It could happen that any savings you realize in a time-share situation might be eaten up by transportation costs there and back.

■ Can you say for sure that you will be free to vacation during the same week or the same season every year? Will children, work, or other obligations prevent you from taking your time-share vacation? If this is even a remote possibility, check to be sure that the resort you are considering has an exchange program with other time-share resorts.

Time-share units are fully furnished (or equipped, in the case of a yacht), and also provide you with linens, cooking utensils, and tableware. Pack your clothes and your sports equipment, and you'll be all set.

There will be expenses you'll incur over and above the cost of the time-share. Every resort charges its time-share owners a maintenance or service fee that pays for insurance, taxes, maintenance, and long-term care of the property. If you want maid service during your stay, you will have to pay for that. Obviously your food (whether you decide to eat in or out) will need to be budgeted. And any recreational activities for which there is generally a fee (golf, boating, skiing) must be taken into consideration. Most resorts do have facilities that are open to all members of the community such as a pool, sauna, hot tub, health club, tennis and racquetball courts, and more. But be sure that you find out exactly which facilities are free to those vacationing in the resort, and which can only be used for a fee. You may be pleasantly surprised or sorely disappointed.

LOGISTICS

Buying one week on a yacht or at a time-share resort means that you own a fraction of that time-share property. There are two ways to arrange the purchase of a time-share property. The most popular kind of time-share ownership is permanent and deeded — you receive a deed and title which make you one of many owners of that property. These are known as *fee simple* transactions and they give you some of the tax benefits associated with home ownership as well as the power (and freedom) to rent, will, donate, or sell the property.

The other kind of ownership is known as a *right-to-use* arrangement, which is similar to a lease except that the "rent" for a predetermined number of years is paid in a lump sum at the time you sign the right-to-use contract. There are more owner restrictions in this kind of ownership: some such contracts prohibit you from sub-leasing your time-share property or even from selling your rights to it. At the end of the specified number of years in the contract (anywhere from 12 to 40) the resort regains ownership of that time period. In most cases, a purchase made under a right-to-use sales agreement is cheaper than one made under the fee simple arrangement.

Although you shouldn't rule out *right-to-use* contracts altogether, it is clear that you will have more flexibility in how you enjoy, and eventually dispose of, your property, as well as greater investment protection, under the *fee simple* arrangement.

Two-thirds of time-share owners finance their purchase with a down payment of between 10 and 20 percent. Most banks won't offer a mortgage for a time-share property, but will help you arrange an installment loan that can run from three to seven years depending on how fast you want to pay it off. Many developers can also offer you financing with a local bank that has an interest in the project.

TIME-SHARE EXCHANGES

A distinct advantage of the time-share vacation is that you have the option of exchanging your vacation period for one at a different resort, even at a different time of the year. Many salespeople will offer you this as an enticement, but be careful. Yes, you can exchange your time-share vacation for another one, but the exchange organizations operate independently of the resorts and you have to be flexible as to exactly where and when you want to exchange.

As with any purchase, be sure that the time-share you want to buy belongs to one or more exchange networks. Such an affiliation will be necessary in order for you to enjoy the benefits of time-share swaps.

The procedure is simple: you join an exchange organization by paying a yearly membership fee and then you "bank" your week at least 60 days before it is scheduled. Shortly thereafter you will receive a form on which you will list four to eight resorts in a particular area that you might want to visit. Exchanges must be made for time periods of equal or less popularity, and for accommodations of similar size. You can swap down, but you can't swap up. For example, if you have a two-bedroom condo in Colorado for winter skiing, you can trade it for a condo of the same size at the same time of year in the Florida Keys. But you can't swap a two-bedroom apartment on Nantucket in February for a four-bedroom set-up at the same time in southern California. All time-share exchanges need to be roughly equal to maintain fairness.

If you successfully exchange your time-share you must pay the exchange service a small fee for each week exchanged, as well as an initiation fee, which is often paid by the developer as an incentive for you to sell your original time-share and buy into theirs. The addresses of the two largest time-share exchange organizations will be found in Chapter 23, "Useful Addresses."

Any time-share resort that belongs to an exchange organization is probably more reliable than one that does not because exchange services periodically inspect all the resorts they offer to their clients. Any resort that fails to meet the outlined standards could be dropped from the list of eligible swap resorts.

TIME-SHARE AUCTIONS

If you want to find even bigger bargains in a time-share vacation you can attend an auction for time-share properties. This represents a wonderful opportunity for shrewd buyers to come away with a time-share property for only 40 to 65 percent of the developer's asking price.

Time-share owners and developers approach auctioneers to sell slower-moving properties, but they aren't necessarily less attractive vacations. According to a resort industry magazine, an astonishing 20 percent of the nation's 800,000+ time-share owners hardly ever even darken the door of their time-share property.

It is the seller of a time-share vacation who pays the expenses of such an auction: auctioneers take a commission of about 15 percent and also charge a listing fee based on the minimum bid the seller establishes for his or her property. Most sellers will probably not recover all the money they paid for their time-share vacation, and they certainly won't make a profit, but if you've been smart and thoughtful in buying a time-share vacation from the start you won't need the services of a time-share auctioneer.

What may look like disappointment, or even disaster, for the seller, represents a terrific bargain for the buyer. Most of the people who attend these auctions are experienced time-share vacationeers and buyers: they want to expand or upgrade their time-share properties. When compared with the cost of taking a hotel room or renting a condominium at some of the resorts offered at auction, it becomes clear that the time-share vacation purchased in this way is a very affordable alternative.

The one thing to keep in mind is that you may want later to sell the time-share you bought at auction, and it could be a long and arduous process. If you bought the vacation at a cut rate to begin with, you shouldn't be too disappointed if it won't sell for a while or if you lose a little money.

FRACTIONAL OWNERSHIP

Another option for those looking to buy vacation properties, based in theory on time-sharing, is called *fractional ownership*. Rather than buying a tiny fraction of a resort vacation (such as 1/52 of a year as is typical with time-sharing), fractional ownership offers its owners bigger chunks of the pie. Fractions are sold in quarters or tenths or twelfths, which entitles you to more time at a resort as well as a greater share of its ownership.

Fractional ownership is a fine compromise for anyone who is interested in more than an $8,000 one-week resort vacation, but doesn't have the resources to buy and maintain a $250,000 vacation home. Friends, relatives, business associates, and resort developers can form partnerships or groups which then purchase a vacation property. Each owner buys a fractional share and gets a separate deed and the rights to use the resort and its facilities for a specified number of weeks a year. In some cases the buyer would have a single month which is theirs to do with as he or she wishes. But in cases where the fractions are larger (one-quarter, one-sixth), owners rotate use of the property in order to be fair, especially if it is not a place with year-round vacation potential. Every owner would have a week or two in the off-season, and then access to the property throughout the rest of the year according to a schedule that is agreed to by each of the owners.

Like time-sharing properties, each fractional owner must pay an annual maintenance fee, and perhaps a small weekly fee to use the resort facilities. And, if you choose not to use a week or weeks of your fraction, you can put that time in the rental pool (of which the resort will take a healthy commission — 20 or 30 percent). A further similarity is an exchange program common to time-sharing resorts. If you are a fractional owner in a resort that belongs to an exchange service, you could swap some of your time at another resort if you wish.

Because fractional ownership represents a bigger financial commitment than time-sharing, you are more likely to qualify for a mortgage in a fractional ownership arrangement. And because each fractional owner has made a separate commitment, the bank only has recourse to those individuals who may be delinquent, not to you if you have been dependable.

Fractional ownership is marketed differently than a time-share vacation — the former is represented more for its ownership potential, the latter more as a fixed vacation expense. Whereas marketing costs can run anywhere from 30 to 50 percent for time-share properties, fractional ownership can be marketed for 15 to 25 percent. You cannot reasonably expect to make money when you sell your time-share property, and even though fractional ownership does not have much of a resale history, there are indications that anyone selling a fraction of their share at a popular resort stands to make at least a little money. Marketing costs being smaller, and the amount of ownership being greater, it stands to reason that fractional ownership is a good bet for those who want more than a one-week time-share.

WARNINGS

Before you take on the commitment of a time-share vacation, no matter how attractive the location and how popular the resort, you should *not* buy a time-share as an investment. The industry is still new, and even the experts can't estimate what kind of return you can expect when it comes time to sell. You may not find a real estate broker or developer eager to help you sell your time-share — they'd rather be selling new units. You may even have to assume the responsibility of selling the time-share yourself, but if not, marketing costs and commissions can easily eat up almost 50 percent of your asking price. If you really want to make an investment, it would probably be wiser to buy a vacation home, rental or commercial property — the benefits of which are more predictable, and which accrue directly to you.

Be an intelligent consumer. Time-sharing has a bad name because of criminals posing as legitimate salespeople who take advantage of trusting souls. People have been known to buy a time-share at a resort that doesn't exist or that is already owned by someone else. Salespeople can be misleading. Carefully investigate every aspect of a prospective time-share property — it won't be easy to resell a time-share that doesn't meet your expectations. You will hear horror stories, and no doubt some of them are true; but, if you follow the guidelines below, you should buy a time-share that will be a source of fun and enjoyment for years to come. Before you sign on the dotted line or succumb to sales pressure, consider the following points:

■ The first and most important step is to examine the resort and its facilities yourself. Rent a room or condo for a few nights or a week. Talk to residents or owners to get their honest assessments. Your first impressions or gut reactions are almost always correct — if they are strong in either the positive or negative range, you know what to do next.

■ Ask about the developer/seller's reputation. Was the building contractor experienced; is the quality of the contractor's work obvious? Do they belong to the National Timesharing Council, which has set ethical standards for its members? Get a copy of the developer's prospectus (their plans for the future); if the long-range goals are for reasonable and attractive growth, that's a good sign. Some states require the developer by law to supply this information to prospective owners.

■ Don't buy a time-share at a facility that is not completed unless you have every assurance from the developer, other owners, and the bank which has financed the resort that the work will be completed. Less than scrupulous developers have been known to sell time-shares to unfinished projects in order to raise the needed capital, only to have the whole thing go into bankruptcy. Be very cautious about buying into a resort that is clearly not finished and not established. If you're sold on an uncompleted resort, it might be a good idea to have your money held in escrow until all the work is finished.

■ Determine whether your contract assigns you to a particular unit or whether the resort will assign you to a different spot every year.

■ Ask that a *nondisturbance clause* be written into your time-share contract. This means that if a resort development defaults on their obligation to the bank, you will retain the right to use your unit.

■ Any oral agreements or promises should always be written into your contract — don't trust that this will happen, insist that they be written in.

■ Check the provisions in your contract about the maintenance fee. Get a written breakdown of maintenance expenses so you can see exactly where the money is being spent. As if there are any limits to its costs — will it increase every year by 20 percent? A portion of every maintenance fee should be set aside for major repairs and capital expenditures; otherwise you could be hit with a big assessment later when facilities have fallen into a state of disrepair.

■ Be careful to buy in an area that is not likely to be grossly overbuilt (just for your protection and privacy). An island resort can become victim to overbuilding, as can very, very popular resorts that may eventually be limited by local zoning regulations.

■ Keep in mind that many exchange programs can't be guaranteed, but if the resort you choose belongs to a recognized exchange service chances are good that you will be able to take advantage of this option.

■ Buy one or two-bedroom units during peak season. Properties of this size and at popular times of the year are both easier to swap for other time-shares and will be easier to sell when the time comes.

■ The *fee simple* purchase arrangement is usually preferable to the *right-to-use* method for the reasons we have outlined above.

■ If you buy under a *fee simple* arrangement, it has been recommended that you may not pay more than ten times the asking rate for a week at a nearby hotel or apartment. A similar calculation for *right-to-use* sales can be made by dividing the number of years by the price paid; the amount you get should not be significantly more than the amount paid for a comparable rental.

■ Don't succumb to any "sign now" pressure, and be wary of promotions that promise you money or prizes just for listening to the sales presentations. More often than not, you will be pestered, harassed, and haggled into signing something you may regret later. There is no need to be intimidated into buying a property you only came to investigate. Be strong. Sales people will tell you that you may miss your chance unless you act soon, but with over 1,000 time-share resorts in the United States, you have plenty of choices.

HOME EXCHANGES

One vacation option that has its roots in the world of academia is that of house swapping, or home exchanging. Originally intended to make the logistics of a visiting professorship easier and more attractive, the idea has gained popularity with those of every travel tendency.

The main reason to choose a house exchange is generally money (the savings are significant compared to a standard vacation). In addition, if you wish to have a total experience in a different place, culture, or lifestyle, there's no better way than to live there.

The idea is quite simple: you exchange your home (and everything your home and your area have to offer) for a home in a place you would like to visit. There are a number of organizations that will advertise your home, match you with a suitable and acceptable exchange situation, and help make the formal arrangements. For these services you pay a modest annual membership fee.

A home exchange vacation can save you thousands of dollars when you consider the costs you would have paid for accommodations, transportation needs, meals, cleaning services, entertainment, and many other hidden expenses. You are usually entitled to use the car, appliances, and recreational facilities that belong to the home you are staying in; the same applies to the people who are staying in your home.

Experienced home exchangers will tell you that the greatest pleasures in home exchanging are not tangible. As a member of a residential community you will experience anew those things that are very much routine at home — food shopping, taking your children to the park, going to the theater, exploring the neighborhood.

If money and new experiences aren't enough to convince you, consider these points:

■ Home exchanges are ideal for those who have families in distant towns. With a home exchange you won't be an imposition and you won't have to spend a fortune on hotels.

■ Retirees and those on tight vacation budgets will find that the home exchange vacation will save money and give you the freedom that a conventional vacation may not allow.

■ Prospective retirees can use house swaps to check out retirement areas before making any big decisions or financial commitments.

■ Children, grandchildren, pets, bikes, and toys are as welcome at an exchange home as at your own home — provided they give your exchange home the same respect you ask at yours.

There are **risks** to house swapping. A home may not be as clean as you might have expected, or the area not as inviting. Even more disappointing is when commitments that were thought to be firm are withdrawn. Even if a better offer comes along, don't cancel your exchange — you wouldn't want someone to do that to you. If you find that you absolutely cannot participate in a planned house exchange for legitimate reasons try to find another couple or family to take your place.

To find out more about house exchanging, write to one of the house exchange organizations listed in Chapter 23, "Useful Addresses." They will send you application forms, subscription prices, and a description of where available houses are located.

These agencies provide neither real estate nor travel services. They compile directories of families seeking holiday home exchanges with others. Almost every other formality of the actual exchange is the responsibility of the subscribing parties.

CHAPTER TWENTY-ONE

TRAVELING ON BUSINESS

Business travelers have different priorities, and more need of genuine savvy, than recreational travelers do. You need to get places fast, economically, efficiently; your travel arrangements and connections must be smooth enough so as not to distract you from the primary focus of your trip.

The business traveler is the bread and butter of the travel industry — you put in the long miles, the numerous nights in hotels, and the business meals at all hours of the day or night.

Because it is too often assumed that the business traveler is working with a fat travel budget, it is harder to find bargain rates and attractive discounts on hotels in particular. The key to finding the best rate for business travel arrangements is flexibility and some intelligent probing.

Develop a good relationship with a travel agency that has a business travel expert who can find you the cheapest and fastest flight, a decent and convenient room that won't bankrupt you, and a rental car without hassles.

If you feel it's impossible to get the service or savings you need through a travel agent, you may wish to train someone in your firm to handle travel arrangements. This person will need toll-free reservation numbers (available through 800-555-1212), a pad of paper, some time to spend, and the combination of patience and persistence that always wins the best deal.

Be sure to plan your route with an eye on **weather conditions.** If you want to go to Las Vegas, and you have a choice of going via Chicago or via Atlanta, take into account possible weather-related delays.

Always **ask for the corporate discount,** and double-check when you pick up your room key or rental car. It's always best to have asked at the beginning of the transaction than at the end.

A relative who spends a good deal of time on the road for business recommends that you save the **plastic bags** your clothes come home from the dry cleaner in. When laying out the clothes for your trip, separate out everything that is easily wrinkled — fine cotton, silks, woolens, and delicate fabrics. Put one or two of these items on a hanger, cover them with a dry cleaner's bag, and pack them in your luggage on the hanger. The plastic prevents wrinkles, and all you have to do when you arrive is reach into your suitcase and hang up your clothes!

Bring a **second pair** of comfortable shoes if you'll be on your feet for more than one day, as, for example, at a trade show.

Take **multiple vitamins** along with you.

TAXES

Under the **Tax Reform Act of 1986,** business meals and entertainment expenses are 80 percent deductible. These expenses may be deducted when they are "ordinary and necessary" to conducting business, not just "good will." The IRS will need full documentation on meal and entertainment expenses, including what is discussed at the time.

Tax experts recommend that you keep **two sets of books** —one for expenses that are fully deductible, and one for those that are 80 percent deductible.

To save money, **take your client to breakfast,** not to lunch or dinner.

AIRLINES

(See Airline Reservation Checklist, Chapter 22.)

Get price quotes from at least three different airlines. Don't forget to check with Canadian airlines, which, in our experience, offer very competitive fares.

If you travel a good deal on business, join a **frequent flyer club** or two. The airline will give you an account number and keep a log of the miles you fly with them. When you reach a certain number of miles the airline will reward you with a bonus — for example, after 20,000 they may give you a free "upgrade" from coach to first class; after 30,000 a free ticket, and so on. Now hotels and rental car agencies have gotten into the act, as well — after you've flown a certain number of miles you may be able to rent a car with unlimited mileage, for example, or a free hotel room.

If you are married, **both you and your spouse** should join frequent flyer clubs, for added discounts.

TIPS TO MAXIMIZE FREQUENT FLYER BENEFITS

■ When choosing a frequent flyer program, consider the airlines that fly into the areas you're most likely to go to.

■ Find out what the minimum prize level is — for some it's 10,000 miles; for others it's 20,000. Western Airlines, at this writing, will upgrade you to first class after you've flown just 500 miles.

■ Tie-ins with hotels and car rental agencies yield lucrative points. Use these associated companies.

■ Keep your own record of the number of miles you've flown. Some travelers find errors in the log the airline supplies.

■ Have your spouse and any traveling children (college or boarding school students) join the program as well.

Always plan to arrive **the night before** your meeting, and earlier if you'll be coping with jet lag.

Avoid scheduling a meeting in Hong Kong followed two days later by a meeting in Paris, or one in San Francisco followed closely by one in New York. You'll be able to make the meetings, but your performance will be seriously hampered by jet lag. See Chapter 7 for information on jet lag.

If you must make several meetings in different parts of the world, try remaining on home-town time throughout the trip. This is the technique made famous by President Lyndon Johnson on political trips around the world.

When you make your flight reservation, get your **seat assignment** as early as possible. Most business travelers prefer a seat on the aisle far up front in the aircraft, so that they can get off the plane quickly after landing. If you are flying on a small commuter plane, especially, sit next to the door. Most or all of your fellow passengers will be business travelers and will race for the first available cabs.

On full-sized aircraft, bulkhead seats have the most room for spreading out your work. Be forewarned, however, that these seats are often assigned to parents traveling with children. If you have a low tolerance for crying babies, you'd better sit farther back or take along some ear plugs!

You can purchase a **pocket airport guide** with diagrams for more than 75 major U.S. airports, showing locations of ticket counters, gates, baggage claims, and car rentals, from AM Data Services, 67 S. Bedford St., Burlington, MA 01803. Call 617-229-5853 for current price.

Because you need to travel fast and light, **avoid luggage check-in** wherever possible. Use a foldover garment bag, which can carry socks and shoes as well as suits, and a briefcase big enough to hold a toilet kit. Your garment bag can be carried on board and hung in a cabinet, rather than checked with other luggage.

Always carry your briefcase, presentation, and slides **on the plane** with you.

Bring in your briefcase a **mini-desk set,** containing scissors, clips, Scotch tape, stapler, calculator, dictation unit, and any other items you frequently use.

If you will be away for more than a few days, **take a shuttle or limousine service** to the airport, rather than using the airport parking lot.

If a shuttle or limousine is not available, find a **Park and Ride** service. Most hotels in the vicinity of airports now offer this service. This may be not only cheaper but also faster than the airport's long-term lot. The service will deliver you at your departure gate and pick you up at the baggage claim area. Some of these companies even have your car started, cleared, and warmed up in winter months — a real bonus.

Before leaving for the terminal, **telephone the airline** to see if your flight is on time.

At the first sign that your flight may be held up or delayed, if this will create a problem for you, don't waste time standing in line at the ticket counter. **Find the nearest phone.** First telephone your own airline (use its 800 number or a courtesy phone) and ask what the story is and when your flight will leave. Then, if necessary, make inquiries with other airlines to see if you can get on another flight that will be leaving directly.

CAR RENTAL

(See Car Rental Checklist, Chapter 22.)

Ask the agent for their **best deal** or you won't get it.

Ask the agent **where the lot is** in relation to your terminal. Find out if there is a regular shuttle service between the lot and the terminal.

Check your own **personal and corporate insurance coverage** before paying for costly insurance on a rental car. You may already be adequately covered.

Before accepting a rental car, **inspect the vehicle** completely for possible undetected damage that could be charged to you upon return. Should you spot any problem, be sure the agent notes it on the rental agreement.

When you return a rental car to an airport terminal, if you do have luggage to check, **check the bags at curbside** before taking the car back to the parking lot. Double-check that your bags are properly labeled and tagged, take out any carry-on items, return the car to the correct lot, and take a shuttle back to the terminal.

HOTELS

(See Hotel Reservation Checklist, Chapter 22.)

When looking for a hotel, look for convenience, shuttle service to and from the airport, quiet, cleanliness, price, extended room service hours. Check out the new inexpensive chains designed for the business traveler.

Ask what kind of **recreational facilities** the hotel offers — swimming pool, exercise studio, spa, or tennis court — to help pick you up after a long flight or unwind after a stressful meeting.

When making a reservation, ask if there are **popular restaurants and theatres** within walking or cab distance. Entertainment can be an important element of a successful business trip.

When you check in at a hotel, ask if they offer **express check-out service**. This can be a big timesaver, but you will not see the bill until you get home. You simply drop off your room key at a designated place. This will prompt computation of your bill, which will be mailed to your business address. Any problems with the bill must be settled through the mail or over the phone.

Always **examine your hotel bill** carefully, either when you check out or, in the above case, when you receive the bill in the mail.

If you charge services to your hotel room, you can quickly **verify the bill's accuracy** with the following system. Add a tip or arrange the final charges so that the last digit always ends in the same number. For example, let's say you use "4" as the code number. If you have drinks at the bar, add a tip so that the total comes out to $15.54. If you get room service, add a tip so that the charges add up to $10.34; or add a few pennies to your parking charges so that the cost will be $22.04. When you scan your bill at the end of your stay it will be immediately apparent which services you actually charged.

GIVE FEEDBACK

An experienced business traveler has contact with more travel-related personnel and services than any other type of traveler. When you receive exceptional service — either good or bad — do not hesitate to put your thoughts down in a letter to the customer service director. You can get this person's name by calling the firm's toll-free number, asking for the number of the customer service department, and then calling that number for the director's name and correct address. Explain in your letter the circumstances of your trip. You can generally expect a prompt and courteous response.

If the service was very good, a letter of commendation is one of the nicest gestures one professional person can make for another. But if you were mistreated or your accommodations were unsatisfactory, that will be acknowledged in the reply, and some kind of compensation will undoubtedly be made to restore your faith in the company and their product.

CHAPTER TWENTY-TWO

CHECKLISTS

This chapter consists of a number of checklists to help you with your planning. We have found it very helpful to keep all important information together in one place. You may wish to add things to these checklists that you feel are important, and ignore items that don't concern you.

QUESTIONS TO ASK WHEN
MAKING AIRPLANE RESERVATIONS

Is that the lowest fare? Are alternative seatings available and cheaper?
Will I get a better fare if I fly midweek or Saturday?
Is there a corporate rate?
Is there a discount available for: frequent flyers? retired persons? students? children? military?
Is that the only airline serving this airport?
Are there any good standby possibilities?
Would it be cheaper to fly into or out of an adjacent airport?
What are the restrictions — When do I need to make my reservation? purchase my ticket? Is there a penalty if I cancel?
Is it a nonstop flight? direct? What are the stops and how long will they be? If it is a connecting flight, do I have at least 45 minutes to make my connection?
What are the flight numbers?
What type of aircraft is it?
May I have my seat assignment now? Aisle _____ ; Window _____ ;
    Smoking _____ ; Non-Smoking _____ ; Far Forward _____ .
Will a meal be served? Will there be a movie shown?
Note: Write down the name of the clerk, the date, and the time.

10 QUESTIONS TO ASK BEFORE RENTING A CAR?

What's the best deal you have? The best weekend deal? Any specials this week?

What is the mileage charge?

Can the car be picked up at the airport? Where is the lot in relation to the terminal? Is there a shuttle service to and from the terminal?

Can the car be dropped off at the airport? Can it be dropped off in another city, and if so, is there a charge for this?

Is there a corporate rate?

How much for insurance (total)? Will my own insurance policy cover this?

Is there a special rate for different types of car? For members of certain organizations? For extended travel?

What is the car make and model? Is it a: luxury car? jeep? van? camper?

Does the car have any special features: Air conditioning _____ ; Front-wheel drive _____ ; Infant car seat _____ ; Hand controls or wheelchair ramp _____ ? If it is a station wagon or hatchback, does it have a panel that conceals luggage packed inside?

What is the confirmation number?

Note: If you are renting a car in another country, make sure that there are no age restrictions.

QUESTIONS TO ASK
WHEN MAKING A HOTEL RESERVATION

What is the daily rate? the weekly rate?

Is there a corporate discount? a discount for retired persons? for families?

Is the hotel a participant in any frequent flyer programs?

Is there a surcharge for a single traveler?

Are there any "perks" for frequent guests?

Where is the hotel located — in the business district (convenient to where appointments are)? in a quiet part of town? within walking or cab distance of popular restaurants or theatres? on the beach? near the beach? near the ski slopes?

Does public transportation serve the hotel?

What are the parking arrangements? What is the daily parking rate?

Is there a restaurant in the hotel?

What are the room service hours?

Does the hotel have recreational facilities — pool? hot tub? sauna? fitness? club? tennis court? other?

What are the fire safety precautions? What floor will the room be on?

What is check-out time? Is there an express check-out service?

What is the confirmation number?

SAFETY NUMBERS LIST

PASSPORT(S)

Name	Passport No.	City of Issue	Date

AIRPLANE TICKET(S)

Airline	Flight No.	Date	Time	Ticket No.

TRAVELER'S CHECKS

Issuing Company _____ Emergency Phone No. _____

Denomination	Amount	Number	to

CREDIT CARD(S)

Company	Number	Exp. Date	Emergency Phone No.

HOME-TOWN BANK

Telephone No. _____ Account No. _____

Address: _____

GETTING READY — A CHECKLIST

Every step of preparation for a trip can be exciting, yet all too often things get put off until the last minute, when you're in a mad rush. Here's a schedule to guide you in readying everything for a big trip in plenty of time.

Twelve to three months before departure date (depending on where and how you're going):
— Make plane, boat, and/or train reservations.
— Buy a guidebook or two that focus(es) on the areas you'll visit.
— Start developing your itinerary.
— Inquire about hotel rates and make reservations.
— Obtain an International Certificate of Vaccination from the U.S. Public Health Agency or a passport agency.

Four months before departure date:
— Have passport photos taken.
— Find out about car rental, train passes, other internal travel arrangements.
— Begin learning the language? Purchase a phrasebook or instructional tape.

Three months before departure date:
— Apply for passport and, once you have your passport, visas.
— Schedule an appointment with your physician for four to six weeks before you leave. You'll need a complete physical exam. You should also determine if you need any shots and/or medication.
— Make an appointment for a dental checkup and cleaning.

Two months before departure date:
— Call or write the consulates of the countries or the state tourist departments of the states (listed in Chapter 23, "Useful Addresses") you'll be visiting for tourist information.
— Make a list of the things you'll take with you.
— Begin collecting addresses of people you know living abroad.
— Examine insurance policies. Take out additional coverage if desired. Make sure auto, fire, and other policies are up to date.
— If you need new shoes for the trip, buy them now, and start breaking them in.

One month before departure date:
— If you haven't received your passport and visas by now, you should inquire.
— Order foreign currency ($50-$100 worth) through your bank for your needs upon arrival.

— Call the airline for advance seat assignment.
— Have prescriptions filled for extra glasses, contact lenses, or any medications you might need.
— Have a complete physical examination.
— If you are going to be inoculated against typhoid, you must have your first shot now, and your second shot in four weeks. If you need a yellow fever shot, you may get it now also.
— Make plans to board your pets, have your lawn mowed or driveway plowed, and have your mail picked up.

Two weeks before departure date:

— Contact a reliable neighbor or friend and let them know you'll be gone. Arrange to leave this person your itinerary, car license number, and a house key. Get this person's address and telephone number.
— Double-check all travel arrangements, to make sure you haven't forgotten anything.
— If you are going to have a cholera shot, you may get your first one now. Start taking antimalarial medication as well.

One week before departure date:

— Pick up your traveler's checks.
— Arrange to discontinue newspaper, milk, UPS, and other deliveries until further notice. Arrange for the post office to hold your mail if no one will pick it up for you.
— Inform your police department of when you are leaving and when returning. Let them know a neighbor has your house key.
— Make a trial pack to see if everything fits.
— Get your second cholera shot now.
— Telephone your travel agent to find out when you may pick up your ticket.

Three days before departure date:

— Confirm your international flight.
— Pick up tickets, if possible.

Two days before departure date:

— Gather items to be packed. Make sure everything is clean, has working batteries, and so on. If you're the last-minute type, pack now.

One day before departure date:

— Pack.
— Confirm your domestic flight; reconfirm your international flight if you wish. Write down date, time, and name of agent you speak with.

(continued)

Three hours before departure:
— Call airport to find out whether your flight is on time.

Two to three hours before departure:
— Arrive at airport and check in.

One half-hour before departure:
— Arrive at gate.
— Set watch or alarm clock to destination time.

Bon voyage!

PACKING CHECKLIST

This list is for a recreational trip. Don't bring everything listed here — just those items that make sense to you. We consider this amount of things to be packing light, but not extra-light. See Chapter 5, "What to Take," for the latter.

Clothes

2 pairs pants — at least one sturdy and one that's suitable for dress occasions. Fabric should contain some cotton.
3-4 shirts. If you'll be in the tropics, at least one shirt should be long-sleeved to protect against sunburn and mosquitoes. Fabric should contain a fair percentage of cotton.
Sweater — dark color best (wear en route)
One skirt for dress occasions, for comfort en route and in the tropics
One sports jacket for men — some restaurants require them
Swimsuit
Cover-up for beach or pool
Raincoat and galoshes
Hat — beret or sun hat
3-5 pairs underwear
5 pairs socks — cotton or wool
1 pair sturdy, well-broken-in shoes. (Buy sandals in the tropics, walking shoes in Ireland and the U.K., dress shoes in France and Italy.)
Sleepwear

Winter Travel

Down jacket
Boots, well waterproofed
Gloves and hat
Long underwear

Other Essentials — all are small enough to fit in large purse or carry-on

Passport, tickets, itinerary, traveler's checks, yellow health card
Maps
Knife with bottle and can openers and corkscrew (if desired)
Money belt or pouch
Extra glasses, contact lenses, prescriptions
Combination lock
Address book
Day pack — invaluable to carry your things when you take a day trip or leave your bags at Left Luggage; to carry picnics or laundry; to hold camera and film when you pass through security points; as an extra carry-on
Journal
Small pad of paper
Pocket flashlight for each person
Net shopping bag
Traveling alarm clock
Sunglasses
Pens and pencils
Camera, film, batteries, lens covers, lens tissues
Roll of zip-closure bags
Dictionary and/or phrasebook

Laundry Supplies

Laundry detergent in small packets or tubes — Woolite or Prell
Stretchable clothesline with six small clothespins
Small clothesbrush
Inflatable hanger or two
Rubber sink stopper
Plastic bags

First-Aid Kit

Bandages
Moleskin for blisters
Analgesic
Foil-wrapped antiseptic towelettes
Suntan lotion
Insect repellent
Tincture of iodine
Antimalarial pills
Mosquito netting
Thermometer in hard case
Nail clipper
Tweezers

Toilet Articles

Toothbrush and paste, extra dental floss
Soap and soapdish
Shampoo — Prell is good for many different uses
Moisturizer
Lip balm
Small towel and washcloth
Hairbrush and/or comb
Razor, blades, and shaving cream

Optional

Ear plugs and eye shade
Binoculars in hard case
Roll of Scotch tape
Adaptor — but see if you can eliminate any need for it
Transistor radio with extra batteries, or small cassette player
Musical instruments — always a hit when you travel

When Traveling with Infants or Toddlers

Car seat with cloth liner
Disposable diapers
Moist foil-wrapped towelettes
Cloth diaper or two for changing pad
Garbage bags
Diaper rash ointment
Small packets of tissues
Nightlight
Flashlights
Extra juice
Child's cup with drinking spout or collapsible cup
Fork and spoon
Drinking straws
Familiar foods — cereal, crackers, noodles
Finger foods — cubes of cheese, vegetable sticks
Vitamins or fluoride drops
Bibs
Small toys — balloons, figures, miniature cars or trucks, stacking cups,
   playing cards, colored pencils or felt-tip pens, pad of paper
Favorite animal or doll
Pacifier
Compass
Scotch tape
Insect repellent
Baby shampoo and soap
Favorite books

BUSINESS TRAVEL CHECKLIST

Airline	Flight #	Direct?	Non-Stop?	Cost	Departs (city) at (time)	Arrives (city) at (time)

Name of clerk _____ Date & time of reservation _____ Confirmed? _____

Car Rental

Pick up car where? _____ Discount offered? _____ Cost: _____ per day/per week

Shuttle service? _____   Insurance: _____

Drop off car where? _____   Mileage charge: _____

Own insurance policy covers _____   Other charges: _____

                                                              Drop-off fee: + _____

                                                              TOTAL _____

Hotels

Name	Address	Cost Per Day	Restau- rant	Recreational Facilities	Parking	Res. No.	Phone No.

CHAPTER TWENTY-THREE

USEFUL ADDRESSES

Health

Emergency Help

Overseas Citizens' Emergency
   Center
2201 C St. NW
Washington, DC 20520
202-647-5225

Lists of English-Speaking Doctors

International Association for Medical Assistance to Travelers
417 Center St.
Lewiston, NY 14092
716-754-4883

Free. Members receive a directory of
English-speaking physicians who will
provide 24-hour care at reasonable
fees. Includes 450 cities in 116
countries.

Intermedic
777 Third Ave.
New York, NY 10017
212-486-8900

Family membership $10. Lists
English-speaking doctors with fixed
fees in 200 countries.

Emergency Assistance Companies

Access America
600 Third Ave.
Box 807, Fourth Floor
New York, NY 10163
1-800-851-2800

Assist-Card
444 Brickell Ave.
Suite M130
Miami, FL 33131
800-874-2223

Health Care Abroad
243 Church St. W
Vienna, VA 22180
202-393-5500

International SOS Assistance, Inc.
P.O. Box 11568
Philadelphia, PA 19116
215-244-1500

Travel Guard International
1100 CenterPoint Drive
Stevens Point, WI 54481

Obtain information on this service,
underwritten by the Insurance
Company of North America, through
your travel agent. Offers a 24-hour
emergency claims service, emer-

gency assistance, medical expenses, baggage and travel documents coverage, trip cancellation insurance.

Emergency Health Aids
Medic Alert
777 U.N. Plaza
New York, NY 10017

Provides special bracelets and necklaces with emergency information engraved on them.

H.E.L.P.
Box 742505
Houston, TX 77274-9990

On a H.E.L.P. (Help Ensure Life Protection) membership card you have a microfilm insert with your medical history, including allergies, blood type, doctor's name, and so on. Includes stickers to direct attention to the card's location in wallet. Free annual update.

Lifeguard Corporation
Box 15099
Charlotte, NC 28211
800-438-9111

Car decals and iron-on labels alerting emergency personnel to special conditions such as allergies or chronic illnesses.

Passport Agencies

Boston Passport Agency
Room E 123
John F. Kennedy Building
Government Center
Boston, MA 02203

Chicago Passport Agency
Suite 380
Kluczynski Federal Building
230 South Dearborn Street
Chicago, IL 60604

Honolulu Passport Agency
Room C-106, New Federal Building
300 Ala Moana Boulevard
P.O. Box 50185
Honolulu, HI 96850

Houston Passport Agency
1 Allen Center
500 Dallas Street
Houston, TX 77002

Los Angeles Passport Agency
Room 13100
11000 Wilshire Boulevard
Los Angeles, CA 90024

Miami Passport Agency
16th Floor, Federal Office Building
51 S.W. First Avenue
Miami, FL 33130

New Orleans Passport Agency
12005 Postal Services Building
701 Loyola Avenue
New Orleans, LA 70113

New York Passport Agency
Room 270
Rockefeller Center
630 Fifth Avenue
New York, NY 10111

Philadelphia Passport Agency
Room 4426
Federal Building
600 Arch Street
Philadelphia, PA 19106

San Francisco Passport Agency
Suite 200
525 Market Street
San Francisco, CA 94102

Seattle Passport Agency
Room 906, Federal Building
915 Second Avenue
Seattle, WA 98174

Stamford Passport Agency
One Landmark Square
Broad and Atlantic Streets
Stamford, CT 06901

Washington Passport Agency
1425 K Street, NW
Washington, DC 20524

Canadian Passport Office
Ottawa, ONT K1A 0G3

A Canadian passport costs $21.00
and must be renewed every five
years. Obtain a form (Form A for
adults; Form B for children) at any
post office or travel agency. Call 800-
567-9615 for information.

Passport and Visa Service

Passport Plus
677 5th Avenue
5th Floor
New York, NY 10022
800-367-1818
212-759-5540

Discount Travel Services

Stand-Buys, Ltd.
311 West Superior
Chicago, IL 60610
312-943-5737
800-255-0200

Worldwide Discount Travel Club
1674 Meridian Avenue
Suite 304
Miami Beach, FL 33139

Transportation Passes

Forsyth Travel Library
9154 West 57th Street
P.O. Box 2975
Shawnee Mission, KS 66201-1375

Eurailpass
666 Fifth Avenue
6th Floor
New York, NY 10103
212-397-2667

Transportation

Europabus Tours
770 Lexington Avenue
New York, NY 10021
212-751-4200

Europe by Car
1 Rockefeller Plaza
New York, NY 10020
212-581-3040
(in California 213-272-0424)

French Experience
171 Madison Avenue
New York, NY 10016
212-683-2445

Write for information on renting
canal boats.

Useful Organizations

American Association of Retired
  Persons (AARP)
1919 K Street NW
Washington, DC 20049

AARP Travel Service
5855 Green Valley Circle
Culver City, CA 90230
800-227-7737

American Youth Hostels
P.O. Box 37613
Washington, DC 20013-7613
202-783-6161

Several categories of membership —
Senior (ages 18-59); Senior Citizen
(60 and over); Junior (17 and under); 3-Year (ages 18-59); Family
Membership (married couple or
parent (s) with children); Life
Membership (no age limit). With
membership you receive a directory
of U.S. hostels, a quarterly magazine,
and discounts on guide books and
rail passes. The *International Youth
Hostel Handbook* in 2 volumes covers 64 countries with 5,000 hostels.
Volume 1 covers Europe and the
Mediterranean; Volume 2 covers
everywhere else.

At Home Abroad, Inc.
Sutton Town House
405 E. 56th St., 6-H
New York, NY 10022
212-421-9165

Canadian Hosteling Association
National Office
33 River Road
Vanier (Ottawa), ONT K1L 8H9
613-748-5638

Call for addresses of regional offices.

Council on International Educational
    Exchange (CIEE)
205 E. 42nd St.
New York, NY 10017
212-661-1414

Write for International Student Identity Card (also available at CIEE offices in Boston, Seattle, San Francisco, Berkeley, Los Angeles, and San Diego). There is no age limit for this card, but you must be a full-time high school or college student. CIEE also operates low-cost charter flights.

Elderhostel, Inc.
80 Boylston Street
Suite 400
Boston, MA 02116
617-426-7788

If you're 60 or over (or accompanying someone of that age), you can study for two weeks or longer at colleges and universities around the country and around the world. Look for the catalog in your public library.

International Federation of Women's
    Travel Organizations
7432 Caminito Carlotta
San Diego, CA 92120

National Council of Senior Citizens
925 15th Street NW
Washington, DC 20005
202-347-8800

Membership costs $10 a year.

National Retired Teachers Association
1909 K Street NW
Washington, DC 20049
202-872-4700

Membership costs $5 a year.

Rehabilitation International — U.S.A.
20 West 40th St.
New York, NY 10018

Publishes a directory of access guides.

SingleWorld
444 Madison Avenue
New York, NY 10022

This firm offers travel accommodations for people traveling alone.

Travel With Your Children
    (TWYCH)
80 Eighth Ave.
New York, NY 10011
212-206-0688

A resource and information center for parents and travel agents planning family travel. Publishes a monthly newsletter, *Family Travel Times,* as well as two annually updated guidebooks, *Skiing With Children* and *Cruising With Children,* individual travel sheets, and a useful guide to airlines.

Travel Companion Exchange
Box 833
Amityville, NY 11701

A personalized service that carefully matches travel companions of all ages (18 into 80's) and interests.

National Tourism Offices

Antigua Dept. of Tourism
610 Fifth Avenue
New York, NY 10020
1-212-541-4117

Aruba Tourist Bureau
1270 Avenue of Americas
New York, NY 10020
1-212-246-3030
800-TO ARUBA

Australian Tourism Commission
489 Fifth Avenue
New York, NY 10017
212-687-6300

Austrian National Tourist Office
500 Fifth Avenue
New York, NY 10110
212-944-6880

Bahamas Tourist Office
150 E. 52nd Street
New York, NY 10022
212-758-2777

Barbados Tourist Board
800 Second Avenue
New York, NY 10017
212-986-6516
800-221-9831

Bermuda Dept. of Tourism
310 Madison Avenue, Room 201
New York, NY 10017
212-818-9800
800-223-6106

Brazilian Tourism Board
551 Fifth Avenue, Room 421
New York, NY 10176
212-286-9600

British Tourist Authority
(England, Scotland, Wales, N. Ireland)
40 West 57 Street, 3rd Floor
New York, NY 10019
212-581-4700

Bulgarian Tourist Office
161 East 86th Street
New York, NY 10028
212-722-1110

Caribbean Tourism Assn.
20 East 46th Street
New York, NY 10017
212-682-0435

Cayman Island Dept. of Tourism
420 Lexington Avenue
New York, NY 10170
212-682-5582

Colombian Govt. Tourist Office
140 East 57th Street
New York, NY 10022
212-688-0151

Costa Rica Tourist Board
630 Fifth Avenue, Room 244
New York, NY 10111
212-245-6370

Curacao Tourist Board
400 Madison Avenue, Suite 311
New York, NY 10017
212-751-8266

Czechoslovak Travel Bureau
10 East 40th Street, Suite 1902
New York, NY 10016
212-689-9720

Dominican Republic Tourist Information Center
485 Madison Avenue, Suite 205
New York, NY 10022
212-826-0750

Ecuador National Tourist Office
50 E. 40th Street
New York, NY 10003
212-684-3060

Egyptian Govt. Tourist Office
630 Fifth Avenue
New York, NY 10111
212-246-6960

European Travel Commission
630 Fifth Ave., Suite 610
New York, NY 10111

French Govt. Tourist Office
610 Fifth Avenue
New York, NY 10020
212-757-1125

French West Indies
610 Fifth Avenue
New York, NY 10020
212-757-1125

Greek Natl. Tourist Org.
645 Fifth Avenue
New York, NY 10022
212-421-5777

Haiti Govt. Tourist Bureau
630 Fifth Avenue, Suite 2109
New York, NY 10020
212-757-3517

Hong Kong Tourist Assn.
548 Fifth Avenue
New York, NY 10036
212-869-5008

Hungarian Travel Bureau
(IBUSZ)
630 Fifth Avenue
New York, NY 10011
212-582-7412

India Govt. Tourist Office
30 Rockefeller Plaza
New York, NY 10112
212-586-4901

Indonesia Information Office
5 East 68th Street
New York, NY 10021
212-879-0600

Irish Tourist Board
757 3rd Avenue
New York, NY 10017
212-418-0800
800-223-6470

Israel Govt. Tourist Office
350 Fifth Avenue
New York, NY 10118
212-560-0650

Italian Govt. Travel Office
630 Fifth Avenue
Rockefeller Center, Room 1565
New York, NY 10111
212-245-4822 or 4825

Jamaica Tourist Board
866 2nd Avenue, 10th Floor
New York, NY 10017
212-688-7650
800-223-5225

Japan National Tourist Information
630 Fifth Avenue
New York, NY 10111
212-757-5640

Kenya Tourist Office
424 Madison Avenue
New York, NY 10017
212-486-1300

Korea National Tourism Corp.
460 Park Avenue
New York, NY 10022
212-688-7543

Mexican Govt. Tourism Office
405 Park Avenue, Room 1002
New York, NY 10022
212-838-2949

Netherlands National Tourist Office
355 Lexington Avenue, 21st Floor
New York, NY 10017
212-370-7367

. New Zealand Travel Comm.
630 Fifth Avenue, Suite 530
New York, NY 10111
212-586-0060

Philippine Tourism
556 Fifth Avenue
New York, NY 10036
212-575-7915

Puerto Rico Tourism Co.
1290 Avenue of Americas
New York, NY 10104
212-541-6630
800-223-6530

Quebec Govt. House
17 West 50th Street
New York, NY 10020
212-397-0200

Romanian National Tourist Office
573 Third Avenue
New York, NY 10016
212-697-6971

Soviet Union Travel Information Office
630 Fifth Avenue
New York, NY 10011
212-757-3884

Spanish National Tourist Office
665 Fifth Avenue
New York, NY 10022
212-759-8822

Embassy of Sri Lanka
2148 Wyoming Avenue NW
Washington, DC 20008
202-483-4025

Swiss National Tourist Office
608 Fifth Avenue
New York, NY 10020
212-757-5944

Tahiti Tourist Development Board
One Pennsylvania Plaza
New York, NY 10001

Taiwan Visitors Association
One World Trade Center
Suite 8855
New York, NY 10048
212-466-0691

Tourism Authority of Thailand
5 World Trade Center
Suit 2449
New York, NY 10048
212-432-0433

Trinidad and Tobago Tourist Board
400 Madison Avenue
Suite 712
New York, NY 10017
212-838-7750
800-232-0082

Turkish Government Tourism and
  Information Office
821 United Nations Plaza
New York, NY 10017
212-687-2194

U.S. Department of Commerce
United States Travel and Tourism
Room 1524
14th and Constitution Avenue NW
Washington, DC 20230
202-377-3811
202-377-2000

Venezuela Tourist Office
7 East 51st Street
New York, NY 10022
212-355-1101

Customs

U.S. Customs Service
1301 Constitution Avenue NW
Washington, DC 20229-0001
202-566-5285

Government Publications on Travel

These booklets may be ordered from
Department 584R, Consumer Information Center, Pueblo, CO 81009

Access Travel 584R

Design features, facilties, and services for the handicapped at 519 airport terminals in 62 countries. 39
pp. Free.

Fly Rights 148R

How to get the best fares and how to
cope with problems. 32 pp. $1.00.

*Golden Eagle/Golden Age/Golden
  Access Passports* 572R

Information on reduced admission
fees to national parks. 9 pp. Free.

*Guide and Map to the National
  Parks* 149R

Covers nearly 300 parks. $1.25

*Lesser Known Areas of the National
  Park System* 150R

Listing by state of more than 170 national parks. 48 pp. $1.50.

The National Parks: Camping Guide
  152R

A state-by-state listing of 103 parks
with camping facilities. 112 pp.
$3.50.

A Safe Trip Abroad 153R

How to take precautions against and cope with robbery, terrorism, and other dangers. 16 pp. $1.00.

Your Trip Abroad 155R

Tips on international travel, including passports, customs, visas, shots, and insurance. 39 pp. $1.00.

Visa Requirements of Foreign Governments
Bureau of Consular Affairs
CA=PA Room 5807
Department of State
Washington, DC 20520

Send a self-addressed stamped envelope for this publication.

Useful Products

Caswell-Massey
Mail Order Division
111 Eighth Avenue
New York, NY 10011

Traveler's Checklist
Cornwall Bridge Road
Sharon, CT 06069
203-364-0144

Catalog is free to parents traveling with children; 50 cents otherwise. Includes money exchanger/calculator, smoke/burglar alarm, adaptors, etc.

Translator 8000
Langenscheidt Publishers
Maspeth, NY
718-784-0055

Electronic dictionary for French, Spanish or German. Made by Sharp. $69.95.

LS&S Group
800-468-4789

Pocket-sized electronic World-Walker 1 is a "talking translator" that speaks Spanish, French, German or Japanese phrases equivalent to your English. $257.45.

The Orvis Company
Manchester, VT
802-362-3622

Carries many useful travel products, including inflatable neck pillows.

State Tourist Bureaus

Alabama State Bureau of Publicity and Information
532 South Perry Street
Montgomery, AL 36104
800-252-2262

Alaska Office of Tourism
P.O. Box E
Juneau, AK 99811
907-465-2010

Arizona Office of Tourism
480 E. Bethany Home Rd.
Phoenix, AZ 85007
602-255-3618

Arkansas Department of Parks and Tourism
1 Capitol Mall
Little Rock, AR 72201
501-371-1511 or 800-643-8383

California Office of Visitor Services
1121 "L" Street, Suite 103
Sacramento, CA 95814
916-322-1396

Colorado Office of Tourism
1625 Broadway, Suite 1710
Denver, CO 80202
303-866-2205

Connecticut Department of Economic Development
210 Washington Street
Hartford, CT 06106
203-566-3385

Delaware Development Office
99 Kings Highway
P.O. Box 1401
Dover, DE 19903
302-736-4271

Washington D.C. Convention and
Visitors Bureau
Suite 250
1575 Eye St. NW
Washington, DC 20005
202-789-7000

Washington D.C. Tourist Information
Center
1400 Pennsylvania Avenue
Washington, DC
202-789-7000

Florida Division of Tourism
107 W. Gaine Street
Fletcher Blvd., Room 404
Tallahassee, FL 32301
904-487-1462

Georgia Dept. of Industry, Trade and
Tourism
Box 1776
Atlanta, GA 30301
404-656-3545

Hawaii Visitors Bureau
2270 Kalakaua Avenue
Suite 804
Honolulu, HI 96815
808-923-1811

Idaho Division of Tourism
Statehouse
Boise, ID 83720
208-334-2470

Illinois Office of Tourism
620 E. Adams
Springfield, IL 62701
217-782-7139

Indiana Tourism Development
Division
1 N. Capitol, Suite 700
Indianapolis, IN 46204
317-232-8860

Iowa Tourism
200 E. Grand Avenue
Des Moines, IA 50309
515-281-3100

Kansas Dept. of Commerce
400 W. Eighth Street
Fifth Floor
Topeka, KS 66603
913-296-3481

Dept. of Travel Development
Capital Plaza Tower
22nd Floor
Frankfort, KY 40601
502-564-4930

Office of Tourism
P.O. Box 94291
Baton Rouge, LA 70804
504-925-3800

Maine Publicity Bureau
97 Winthrop
Hallowell, ME 04347
207-289-2423

Maryland Office of Tourist Information
45 Calvert Street
Annapolis, MD 21401
301-269-3517

Massachusetts Division of Tourism
Dept. of Commerce & Development
100 Cambridge St.
Boston, MA 02202
617-727-3201

Michigan Travel Bureau
Dept. of Commerce
P.O. Box 30226
Lansing, MI 48909
517-373-1195

Minnesota Office of Tourism
375 Jackson Street
Suite 250
St. Paul, MN 55101
612-296-5029

Mississippi Dept. of Economic
Development
Division of Tourism
Walter Sillers Building
P.O. Box 22825
Jackson, MS 39205

601-359-3414 or
800-647-2290 (out-of-state)
800-962-2346 (in-state)

Missouri Division of Tourism
P.O. Box 1055
Jefferson City, MO 65102
314-751-4133

Dept. of Commerce
Travel Promotion Unit
Helena, MT 59601
406-444-2654

Nebraska Division of Travel and
  Tourism
Dept. of Economic Development
301 Centennial Mall South
P.O. Box 94666
Lincoln, NE 68509
402-471-3796
800-228-4307 (out-of-state)
800-742-7595 (in-state)

Nevada Division of Tourism
Capitol Complex
600 E. Williams
Carson City, NV 89710
702-885-4322

New Hampshire Division of
  Economic Development
Office of Vacation Travel
P.O. Box 856
Concord, NH 03301
603-271-2665

New Jersey Division of Travel and
  Tourism
1 West State, CN 826
Trenton, NJ 08625
609-292-2470

New Mexico Tourism and Travel
  Division
1100 St. Francis Drive
Santa Fe, NM 87503
505-827-0291

New York State Division of Tourism
1 Commerce Plaza
Albany, NY 12245
518-474-4116

North Carolina Travel and Tourism
  Division
430 N. Salisbury Street
Raleigh, NC 27611
919-733-4171

North Dakota Tourism
Capitol Grounds
Bismarck, ND 58505
701-224-2525

Ohio Travel and Tourism
P.O. Box 1001
Columbus, OH 43216
614-466-8844 or 800-848-1300

Oklahoma Division of Tourism
  Promotion
500 Will Rogers Bldg.
Oklahoma City, OK 73105
405-521-2464

Oregon Travel Information Office
595 Cottage Street NE
Salem, OR 97310
503-378-6309

Pennsylvania Travel Bureau
416 Forum Building
Harrisburg, PA 17120
717-787-5453

Rhode Island State Office of Tourism
Dept. of Economic Development
7 Jackson Walkway
Providence, RI 02903
401-277-2601

South Carolina Division of
  Tourism
Box 71
Columbia, SC 29202
803-734-0135

South Dakota Division of Tourism
Capital Lake Plaza
711 Wells Avenue
Pierre, SD 57501
605-773-3301

Tennessee Tourist Development
P.O. Box 23170
Nashville, TN 37203
615-741-2158

Tourist Bureau
Capital Station
c/o Dewett C. Greere Bldg.
11th St. and Brazos
Austin, TX 78701
512-463-8586

Utah Travel Council
Council Hall, Capital Hill
Salt Lake City, UT 84114
801-533-5681
Vermont Travel Division
134 State St.
Montpelier, VT 05602
802-828-3236

Virginia Division of Tourism
202 N. 9th Street
Richmond, VA 23219
804-786-4484

Washington State Tourism Division
101 General Adm. Bldg.
Olympia, WA 98504
206-753-5600

West Virginia Travel Development
   Division
2101 Washington St. E
Third Floor
Charleston, WV 25305
304-348-2286

Wisconsin Division of Tourism
PO Box 7606
Madison, WI 53707
608-266-2161

Wyoming Travel Commission
Frank Norris, Jr., Travel Center
Cheyenne, WY 82002
307-777-7777

Cruises

Cruise Lines International Association
Pier 35, Suite 200
San Francisco, CA 94133

Yours for the asking is an interesting brochure called "Answers to the Most Asked Questions About Cruising."

Cruise Passengers Club International
Box 9
Cynwyd, PA 19004

You can buy their annual ship rating report for $10.

Cruise Travel Magazine
P.O. Box 10139
Des Moines, IA 50340

Subscriptions are available for $12 a year.

Freighters

Freighter Travel Club of America
P.O. Box 12693
Salem, OR 97309

You might be interested to see their monthly newsletter *Freighter Travel News.*

Trav-L-Tips, Freighter Travel Association
163-09 Depot Road
Flushing, NY 11358

For a modest membership fee, you are entitled to a bimonthly publication and book services. Just write for more information.

Ford's Freighter Travel Guide
P.O. Box 505
Woodland Hills, CA 91365

A new and updated edition of this publication is available twice a year. Write to ask the cost for the book and postage and handling.

The most common shipping lines in freighter travel are Polish Ocean

Lines, Prudential Lines, Lykes Brothers, and American President Lines. Ask your travel agent for addresses and phone numbers of these organizations.

Discount Travel International Club
7563 Haverford Avenue
Philadelphia, PA 19151

Professional Home Sitters

Home Sitting Services, Inc.
3000 South Jamaica Court
Suite 225
Aurora, CO 80014

They will hire responsible adults to live in your home 24 a hours a day and provide total care and security. Just write for more information.

In An Emergency/Going By Plane

Civil Aeronautics Board
90 Church Street
Room 1316
New York, NY 10007

Their booklet "Fly Rights" will give you all the passenger information you need on how to deal with lost or damaged luggage and other airline emergencies.

Vacation Rentals

(The first two only provide a listing of rentals in foreign countries.)

At Home Abroad
405 East 56th Street
New York, NY 10022

Villas International
213 East 38th Street
New York, NY 10016

Interhome, Inc.
297 Knollwood Road
White Plains, NY 10607

Home Exchanging or Swapping

Vacation Exchange Club, Inc.
12006 111th Avenue, Suite 12
Youngstown, AZ 85363

Time-Sharing

National Timesharing Council
1000 16th Street NW, Suite 604
Washington, DC 20036

The two organizations below offer time-share exchange services.

Resort Condominiums International
P.O. Box 80229
Indianapolis, IN 42680

Has 700 resorts in more than 30 countries.

Interval International
P.O. Box 1380
Buffalo, NY 14205

Has 400 resorts in more than 30 countries.
or
P.O. Box 4301920
7000 SW, 62nd Avenue
Suite 306
South Miami, FL 33143

Travel Information Services

Travel Quest
20103 La Roda Court
Cupertino, CA 95014
408-446-0600

Tour Search™ lists special interest tours around the world. Traveler's Book Match™ lists books by subject and region. Quarterly newsletter. Membership $65 per year.

INDEX

209

checklist, 192
children's, 154, 160
cruise, 78-79
older travelers, 164
for temperature extremes, 38
travel, 44-45
walking, 93
Club Med, 147
Coffee, and diarrhea, 26
Comfort
on airplanes, 62-65
on trains, 90
Condoms, 29
Constipation, 26-27
Consumer Information Center, 167, 203
Contact lenses, 20, 40
Continental breakfasts, 99
Corporate discounts, 180
Council on International Educational Exchange (CIEE), 90, 200
Courier service runners, 53
Credit cards, 16-17
and hospitals, 31
lost, 132
and shopping, 116
Criminal offenses, 132
Cruises, 74-77
addresses, 207
for older travelers, 163
special, 82-83
Culture shock, on returning home, 139
Currency
converting to U.S. dollars, 15, 18
foreign, 15
Customs
children's manners, 152
local, 111
table manners, 105
Customs, U.S., 135, 203
after cruises, 81
registering cameras, 119

D

Debarkation procedures, on cruises, 81
Dehydration, and jet lag, 68
Demi-pension, 99-100
Dental exam, 20
Developing film, 123-124
Diaper changing, on airplanes, 44, 159
Diarrhea, 25-26, 27, 139
Dictionaries, 113
Diners Club International, 17
Dining, 103-107. *See also* Restaurants
in France, 106
solo travelers, 145-146
women travelers, 145-146

Disabled travelers, 165-167
bus discounts, 92
on cruises, 82-83
and public transportation in Europe, 93
and seat selection on airplanes, 55
Discount Travel International Club, 208
Discount travel operators, 52, 199
Discounts
air travel, 51-52, 181
bus travel, 92
corporate, 180
cruises, 75-76
for older travelers, 163-164, 165
train travel, 89-90
Diseases. *See also* specific diseases
immunizations against, 21
sexually transmitted, 29
Doctors. *See* Physicians
Documents, 7-12. *See also* Passports
for cruises, 77
list, 10
protecting, 128
Dogs, guide and hearing, 166
Driver's license, international, 10
Driving, 10, 85-88. *See also* Car travel
abroad, 85
and drinking, 132
and solo travelers, 147
in the U.S., 85
Dry skin, 44
in airplanes, 64
Duties, 116, 135-137
exemptions, 118
on items mailed to the U.S., 138
Duty-free allowance, 116
Duty-free gifts, 65
Duty-free items, 136
Duty-free shops, 117

E

Earaches, and infants on airplanes, 159
Eating. *See also* Dining; Restaurants
with chopsticks, 105
with fingers, 105
Emergencies, 130-133
Ehret, Dr. Charles F., 68
Elderhostel, 165, 200
Elderly travelers. *See* Older travelers
Electronic translators, 114
Emergency assistance insurance plan, 32
Emergency help, 130-133, 197
Enterovioform, 26, 31
Eurailpass, 89-90
and ferries, 92, 110
and steamer travel, 92
Europe by Car, 86
European hotels, 98

reservations
  for disabled travelers, 167
  questions to ask, 188
  reconfirming, 49-50
  safety, 128-129, 144-145
  U.S., 100
  women travelers in, 144-145
House sitters, 208
House swapping. *See* Home exchanges
Hygiene, personal, 28-29

I

Ice cream, 24
Illness, 31. *See also* specific diseases
Immunizations, 20-22
"Importing a Car", 137
Infants. *See* Children
Information on restaurants, 104
Injuries, 31
Inoculations. *See* Immunizations, 20
Insects, 29-30
Insurance, 31-33
  cancellation, for air travel, 57
  corporate, for rental cars, 183
  countries not covered by most policies, 33
  excess valuation coverage, 71
  new cars in Europe, 87
  older travelers, 165
  personal, for rental cars, 183
  and robberies, 132
  trip, 77
Intermedic, 197
International Association for Medical
    Assistance to Travelers, 197
Interantional Driving License, 10, 85-86
International Federation of Women's Travel
    Organizations (IFWTO), 107, 200
International Funds Transfer Service, 131
International highway signs, 20, 88
International telephone calls, 11
International Youth Hostel Handbook, 101,
    199
International Youth Hostel Organization,
    90
Iodine, for treating water, 23
Ireland
  meals, 103
  reservation service, 100

J

Jet lag, 67-68, 181
  and skiing, 30-31
Jewelry, 37
Journal writing, 141

K

Knife, folding, 39-40
"Know Before You Go", 116, 135

L

Labels for suitcases, 42
Language, 113-114
  and children, 152
Laundry
  services in Third World countries, 36-37
  supplies, 40
    checklist, 193
Leasing cars in Europe, 86-87. *See also*
    Rental cars
Lenses, camera, 120
  haze filter, 121
License to drive, 85-86
  international, 10
Liquids, packing, 42
Lodging, 97-102. *See also* specific types
  reservation service, 100
  U.S., 100
  with children, 151-152
Lomotil, 26
London, intercity travel vouchers, 92
Lost credit cards, 132
Lost passport, 131
Lost traveler's checks, 132
Luggage, 36, 41-43, 59-61
  business travelers, 182, 183
  and car travel, 86
  carry-on, 20, 43, 44-45
  on a cruise, 79
  forwarding by trains, 91
  lost by airlines, 70-72
  older traveler's, 164
  problems, 133
  protecting, 127
  storage at train stations, 91
Lunch, 103, 146

M

Mail
  international, 11-12
  Remittance Orders, 131
  in Third World countries, 12
  to the U.S., 138
Malaria, 21-22
  precautions against, 29
Manners, 105-106
  children's, 152
Maps, 38, 92
  for children, 154-155
MasterCard Gold credit cards, 17
Meals on a cruise, 79-80
Measles, 22
Medic Alert bracelet, 20